Mischief in the Mountains

STRANGE
TALES OF
VERMONT
AND
VERMONTERS

Mischief
in the Mountains

EDITED BY
Walter R. Hard, Jr.
Janet C. Greene

ILLUSTRATED BY
Jane Clark Brown

VERMONT LIFE MAGAZINE
MONTPELIER, VERMONT

Published by *Vermont Life* Magazine, Montpelier, Vermont.
Distributed outside of Vermont by
The Stephen Greene Press, Brattleboro, Vermont.

Library of Congress Catalog Card Number: 78–117724
International Standard Book Number: 0–8289–0117–1

Designed by Linda Dean Paradee

Manufactured in the United States of America

For special assistance given in the preparation of the stories and the illustrations contained in this book, warm appreciation is extended by the editors to Mr. Floyd Butler, Mr. Alan Cooke, Mr. J. Stott Dawson, Mrs. John T. Morton, Miss Violene Parker, Mr. Roland Wells Robbins, the Shelburne Museum and the Vermont Historical Society.

Contents

Prologue

TALES OF THE BAROQUE, the true and the apocryphal, have always had a great appeal to the Vermonter, perhaps to compensate for his toilsome daily existence, and partly because of the element of ambivalence in his individualism. Although he may proudly identify with such God-fearing, law-abiding, monosyllabic fellow natives as Calvin Coolidge, he relishes vicariously the recklessness of a flamboyant Vermonter like "Jubilee Jim" Fisk, who finagled the Erie Railroad away from none other than Commodore Vanderbilt, almost cornered the gold market, triggered the Black Friday panic of 1869, and was shot to death in a jealous quarrel over the favors of the glamorous New York actress Josie Mansfield. And eminent native-son philosopher John Dewey does not stir the excitement aroused by the memory of that other Vermont Dewey, Admiral George, who went from Montpelier to destroy the Spanish fleet at Manila Bay.

Another Vermonter who did not fit the "typical" mold was Horace A. W. Tabor, who deserted his Holland, Vermont, birthplace, trekked to Colorado, and won a fortune in the mines and the sobriquet "Silver Dollar." Tabor got himself appointed United States Senator for thirty days, divorced the wife who had crossed the Plains with him, and married blue-eyed "Baby Doe" McCourt, thirty years his junior, in a gaudy and expensive Washington wedding attended by the President of the United States, Chester A. Arthur of Fairfield, Vermont. Although Baby Doe was from Wisconsin, she lived and died in the Vermont tradition of her husband — and of these tales. Wearing a $90,000 diamond necklace when she married, she perished in poverty, frozen to death in the shafthouse of one of Tabor's played-out mines.

9

Vermonters were not alone in their fascination with the weird, the grotesque and the mysterious. Similar nineteenth century tastes were not even confined to America, for by the end of the century Edgar Allan Poe's influence had spread to Europe; the *fin de siècle* saw the emergence in England of Conan Doyle's Sherlock Holmes, Wilkie Collins's *The Woman in White* and Hornung's Raffles, while in France Maurice Leblanc gave birth to Arsène Lupin, a Gallic version of Raffles.

The Raffles-Lupin characterization, the bandit with the heart of gold, had long been a favorite in folklore. However, the inside-out Robin Hood — the wolf-in-sheep's-clothing type of scoundrel — came along much later. The classic example of this dichotomous personification of good and evil, Stevenson's *Dr. Jekyll and Mr. Hyde*, appeared only in 1886, the same year that Clarence Adams, Vermont's own true-life gentleman burglar, began his long, felonious career.

Bristol Bill Warburton, the courtly counterfeiter, was open for business in northeast Vermont thirty-six years earlier. Bristol Bill, however, although pardoned a few days after being found guilty for the third time, ended his story prosaically by dropping out of sight as became a proper Britisher. Adams, on the other hand, prolonged the mystery of his double life beyond his putative death. In the true Vermont manner he deserves a place among such real-life lawless folk heroes as Mike Fink, the legendary rip-roarer of the Mississippi boatmen.

Poe's "Ms. Found in a Bottle" predates by twenty years the discovery of "Johne Graye's" message found in a lead tube on the banks of the Missisquoi. Poe's unfortunate sailor, by the way, takes four thousand words to tell his sad story, whereas Graye, with typical Vermont economy of style, needs only forty to describe his own tragic situation.

Poe could very well have invented Farmer Morse's deep-frozen folk, not only because it was in his own grisly vein, but because he delighted in fooling people as much as Allen Morse did. He would have loved the Woodstock vampire, and it is possible that he did love the story of Mercie Dale's curse on the Hayden family, that doomed clan with such fascinating names as Silence, Azuba, Alvina, Arathuza and Armenia Mamie, but it is not probable. Although Mercie Dale pronounced her dying malediction upon the House of Hayden nine years before the House of Usher appeared in print, Poe did not live to see her witchcraft work its way through the three generations.

One case that is more in the province of Sigmund Freud than of Poe is that of Stephen Boorn, saved from the gallows by the reappearance of the man he was supposed to have murdered seven years earlier. How Stephen could have put his life in jeopardy by making such a detailed confession of the murder and the disposal of the body, while the "victim" was alive and working in New Jersey, is a question for psychiatrists to answer. They might also look into the matter of Uncle Amos Boorn's lugubrious dream and its gullible acceptability. The fact that the "murder" trial had to be moved from the courthouse to a church in order to accommodate the six hundred bloodthirsty spectators is proof positive (if any is needed) that Vermonters were (and still are) *aficionados* of death and violence at second hand.

But it is time to end this psychological speculation. Let the reader pull up a chair in front of the hearth and, even if it is fireless mid-Summer and he must imagine the shriek of the snow-laden wind outside, settle down to enjoy an exciting evening with these tales of untrammeled Vermonters on their own home ground.

LAWRENCE GOLDTREE BLOCHMAN

New York, N.Y.
January, 1970

Mischief in the Mountains

The Man Who Wouldn't be Bored

STEPHEN GREENE & WALTER HARD, JR.

GREAT MYSTERIES SEEM TO FAVOR obscure beginnings, flourish in quiet settings. What better spot, then, for Vermont's most persistent mystery (and one of its most talented criminals) than the placid town of Chester?

Here, on a September night in 1886, in garish contrast to the otherwise pastoral calm of Green Mountain life, the Adams & David Company was broken into and money was stolen from the safe. Town Constable Henry Bond investigated, of course: various neighborhood ne'er-do-wells were questioned; the amateur sleuths of the area advanced theories, none of them tenable. In sum, the results were nil and the crime remained unsolved.

Thus modestly began a series of burglaries which finally totaled, over a sixteen-year period, better than half a hundred. The usually ingenious and often imaginative crimes baffled the authorities completely, reduced the merchants and others of the residents of Chester to near desperation, and provided vintage crackerbarrel gossip for a generation of county residents.

Adams & David was burgled twice more before it was all over. But so was nearly every other store on Main Street. Ware & Sons, Waterman's Mill, and Burditt Brothers, which all sold farmers' supplies, were entered repeatedly with intent to commit a felony. Bundles of shingles disappeared from the station freight yard; a $75 bicycle — one of the stylish new "safety" bikes with same-sized wheels — was spirited through the broken window of Walker's Furniture Store; George Allen, a prosperous farmer, lost $1,500 in cash realized in a Boston cattle deal. (He and his wife jerked awake one night to stare into the barrel of a gun held by a masked bandit whose colleague was ransacking the house. A

15

cordon was thrown around the village and a posse combed the wooded areas, but without success.) Neighboring communities, such as North Springfield, were sometimes victimized, but most of the crimes occurred in Chester.

· James E. Pollard, who owned perhaps the largest general store in town, was particularly favored by the homegrown burglar with the daredevil streak and a taste for anything portable: his place was broken into no less than six times in the sixteen years. Even when Pollard installed a fancy burglar alarm, the thief entered the next night through a 14″ x 18″ closet window (the only aperture that had not been wired) and made off with a fur coat, a woman's cape and fifteen dollars.

Nothing that anyone did seemed to make any difference, except, perhaps, to act as a goad. There was no State Police force in those days and the real responsibility for the town's security rested in the hands of the Board of Selectmen. They did their best. After $500 was offered as reward money, First Selectman Clarence Adams added another $100 from his own pocket. At one point the selectmen imported a detective from Boston. (The gum-shoe turned out to be an amiable lush: the only things he uncovered were several sources of liquor in supposedly dry Chester.) And when druggist F. W. Pierce brought in some revolvers to supply the townspeople it wasn't long before the prowler took up the challenge. He jimmied his way into Pierce's Store and took all the guns that were left.

There were a number of suspects, of course, during this period. Young Gideon Lee was one of them. Lee had been involved in several scrapes, but he died soon afterward, and Chester's crime wave continued unabated. Similarly, one Thomas Converse was suspected of the thefts following his arrest elsewhere in Windsor County. But Converse died at the county jail in Woodstock — and the burglaries continued.

One of the most frequent sufferers was Charles H. Waterman, owner and operator of the gristmill located on the bank of the river just north of Chester Depot, who kept losing bags of feed. Try as he would, he could never figure out how the marauder got into his mill. Finally he deduced from some slight scratches that the burglar would remove the locks from the mill doors completely, then replace them after making his haul. Former selectman Clarence Adams checked on the repeated breaks with Mr. Waterman and approved the miller's plan to employ a night watchman. This was carried out for a matter of some weeks, and the mill enjoyed a period of quiet. Then the watchman was taken off and the mill breaks started in again.

Over the years, however, Mr. Waterman had noticed something else about Chester's cracksman. He noticed that the burglar was never one to do the obvious, but seemed to favor difficult methods of entry that called for real ingenuity. Following his hunch, Mr. Waterman figured that the burglar's next visit to the mill would be effected through a difficult window which lay on the downstream side near the back. Without telling anyone, he resolved to rig this window with a booby trap.

This window selected by Mr. Waterman was some fifteen feet directly above the raceway of the mill, but it might be reached by an agile man from the roof of an engine shed attached to the main part of the mill. The miller secured a shotgun just inside the window with a string running through hooks to the window's lower sash. If the window was opened the string would tighten against the trigger and the gun would then discharge directly at the opening.

That night, July 29, 1902, Charles Waterman was attending a school board function at the town hall. But his parents and Gardner, his twenty-year-old son, were sitting in the family parlor across the road from the mill. Gardner knew about the trap his father had set; no one else did.

In the middle of the evening they heard a report. "Some of the boys must have some crackers left over from the Fourth," the grandfather commented. But young Gardner was already out the door, running to get his father, and headed across the covered bridge toward the lights in the town hall. As he recalled it later, not far from the town wagon sheds he saw a tall figure lying in the bushes by the road. It was a tramp or a drunk, he thought; he ran on.

Charles Waterman and Gardner hurried back to the mill with Constable Bond. There they found the gun discharged all right and blood on the windowsill, but no thief.

A little later that night, about ten it was, former selectman Clarence Adams was found by an unidentified passer-by lying slumped in the back of his buckboard by the watering trough just below his hilltop farm. His lower clothing was covered with blood, his left leg swung limp and bleeding.

"I've been shot by highwaymen!" he told Mrs. Elmina Walker, his housekeeper, when brought to the house. "Help me to bed and call a doctor." William Dunn of North Springfield, a friend and erstwhile neighbor who happened to be there at the farm that night, went for the doctor.

When Dr. Walter L. Havens, who was also at the town hall, arrived, Adams told him the same story — two men had sprung from the bushes at the side of the road and held him up. He was still in the seat of his buckboard when one of the men shot him.

The wound was a bad one; the flesh had been very substantially shot away from the inside of the left thigh. Dr. Havens said he would bring Dr. John Stevenson in the morning to give the wound the surgical attention it needed. That morning the two doctors removed eighty-four pieces of Number 8 shot from Adams's leg.

As the reader knows well, news in a small town travels with the speed of light. Word flew through Chester that Summer morning in 1902 that two crimes, not just one, had been committed the night before: Waterman's Mill had been entered by burglars — this was nothing new, of course — and not twenty rods from Waterman's, Clarence Adams had been held up and shot — evidently by the same men.

His was the first wound inflicted by the local outlaw, and Town Clerk A. D. L. Herrick voiced the general angry sentiment. "What is the town coming to when honest citizens' lives and their property are at the mercy of a gang of criminals like these?" he demanded.

Adams naturally had the sympathy of the community and Constable Bond was urged to make every effort to apprehend the criminals. So he started by carefully searching Four Corners, near Waterman's Mill where Adams said he had been held up.

And there the constable discovered a strange thing: no footprints or recent marks of any kind scarred the smooth dirt by the road. Somewhat puzzled, he returned to the Adams place and examined the buckboard. He found no blood on the seat, where the selectman said he had been sitting when the shot was fired; there was only the pool of blood on the low platform at the rear of the wagon.

The constable then conferred with Charles Waterman, showing him the shot that had been removed from Adams's leg. The booby-trap gun, Waterman said, had indeed been loaded with Number 8 shot.

That did it. The two men reached the conclusion that has already occurred to the reader. It was the greatest shock that each was to have in his lifetime.

"Why, Mr Adams was here just after my mill was robbed of grain on July third, and he was sorry to hear of my loss," Waterman told a reporter at the time. "And I told him then that I was going to have a watchman for the next two or three weeks. He thought it was a good idea. I had dismissed the watchman on July 25th, and then the plan of placing the spring gun, instead of hiring another watchman, occurred to me. In fact, I should have told Mr. Adams of this yesterday if I had had the chance, because he had been so interested in the matter before."

Mrs. Frank Adams, wife of a distant cousin — there are quite a few people named Adams in Chester — recalled later being told of the news back in 1902. She was visiting in Waterbury at the time and a Waterbury friend told her that the famous Chester Burglar had turned out to be a man named Clarence Adams.

"It isn't Clarence Adams, I know," she remembers telling her informant with complete conviction. "It just couldn't be he. I'm absolutely positive of that."

Mrs. Guy Earle, another contemporary, was equally emphatic about her reaction. "I couldn't believe it. He'd be the last person in the whole town I would expect to be responsible for all those crimes."

Edward Kendall told these reporters that his father had more than once said he hoped that Ed, when he grew up, would make as good a citizen as Clarence Adams was.

Yet there was no room for doubt after the constable, with plenty of volunteers, had poked around the Adams farm for half a day. They found grain sacks from Waterman's. They found the missing shingles — some of them anyway. They found the guns stolen from the drugstore and much of the jewelry that had disappeared, over the years, from Chester homes. They found in the incongruous assortment of loot a whole box of pre-tied bow ties that (they were to learn later) had been stolen from a Montpelier haberdasher the year Adams was up in the legislature. They even found, hanging forlornly in a tree out back, the rusted frame of the new safety bike for which the merchant Walker had once asked $75.

No, there was no doubt of it now: First Citizen Clarence Adams and the by-now famous Chester burglar were, however incredibly, one and the same man.

It was not easy for the residents of Chester — population about two thousand at the time — to accept the fact that their leading citizen was also the state's Public Enemy Number One.

For one thing he was, as they must often have said in those days, an imposing figure of a man. He stood just short of six feet in height and weighed a rugged and wiry one-hundred-and-sixty pounds. He must have had exceptional stamina and vitality, too: the doctors said it was a miracle that a man with such a wound could have successfully got down from the Waterman window and made his way unaided the long half-mile to his buckboard.

He had blue eyes, brown hair and a medium complexion. A bachelor, he dressed well, trimmed his mustache with considerable care, always spoke carefully and to the point. (They said there was no one, come Town Meeting day, who was listened to with more respect.) But Adams was never forbidding — he was a friendly man and, using the word in its nicest sense, something of a politician.

He came from a pioneer Vermont family. His great-grandfather had fought in the Battle of Bunker Hill and his people were collaterally related to the distinguished family which gave two presidents to the nation. Clarence's ancestors had settled in Cavendish, a few miles north of Chester on the Black River, in 1780. Clarence was born there on November 18, 1857, and for some reason was taken at an early age by his parents to the hilltop farm in Chester. In a day when small, family-sized farms were still practical, the Adamses were considered moderately prosperous farmers.

Clarence attended school in Chester, and as a young boy showed unusual interest in travel and literature. He told a contemporary newspaper reporter: "When I was a boy my great desire was to enter the Army or Navy, but circumstances prevented my doing it. My father and mother opposed it. They were growing old and needed my help."

Even as a young man he avoided the frivolous diversions of teenagers of his day, and turned toward reading and study.

His early interest in books ran to adventure and romance. His favorite authors included Conan Doyle, Robert Louis Stevenson, Dickens, Poe, Hugo, and Dumas, and fully half his library (it comprised two thousand volumes in the end) consisted of the detective stories of the period, starring such operatives as Nick Carter and Old Sleuth. Prophetically, one of Adams's most heavily thumbed volumes was his copy of *The Strange Case of Dr. Jekyll and Mr. Hyde*. "That book fascinated me," he commented later.

He wrote a paper published in *The New York Times* literary supplement on "The Appreciation of J. Fennimore Cooper" — or so it is claimed, at any rate, in a Hearst sheet at the time of his trial. And he replied once in the public press to a critic who had attacked the historical romance.

At the age of about twenty-five, Adams wanted to be a detective and tried to get a job in the United States Secret Service. His mother objected to this, however. From his constant reading he early formed a desire to travel. In spite of farm duties and the need to care for his aging parents, he did, according to a 1902 report, take two trips to the West.

It is inevitable that Clarence's misdeeds were later ascribed by some to this unusual interest in books. Reading may well have been considered as socially deviant an activity in Chester in 1900

as Elmo Roper averred that is was throughout America in the 1950's. Mrs. Walker, the Adams's corpulent housekeeper, had had a premonition of trouble: "He used to sit up all hours reading and I often wondered it didn't drive him crazy sooner than it did. Reading is the cause of it all; it has turned the poor man's head."

Still, in spite of his exotic and suspect pastime, Clarence Adams, at the time of his arrest, was the favorite son and leading citizen of Chester. Not only had he served as a founding trustee of the Whiting (town) Library for many years (and chosen the books for that institution during the period); he was also an incorporator of the Chester Savings Bank, the chairman, in 1892, of the Board of Selectmen, and was, for a term, Town Representative to the Vermont General Assembly.

The Grand Jury called to deal with Adams's case could put only one interpretation on the facts: an indictment was issued against him and his bail was fixed at $3,000. Many Chester people — among them Town Clerk Herrick, who had conducted the town's business with Adams for a number of years — refused to believe that his colleague could be in his right mind. If, indeed, he was responsible for the crimes at all. Herrick went bond for the $3,000 and only after a week had passed and when finally convinced of Adams's guilt did he surrender him to the constable.

Adams was still recovering from the gunshot wound when he was taken to Woodstock for trial. Apparently charged only with the Waterman burglary, he pleaded guilty, refused to implicate any confederate in his crimes, was convicted on August 14, 1902, and sentenced to nine to ten years in the State Prison at Windsor. He signed a power of attorney to have his property sold and was committed to Windsor the following day.

On March 5, 1904, the following notice appeared in the *Vermont Journal*:

Clarence A. Adams, the gentleman burglar from Chester, who was serving a ten years' sentence in the State Prison at Windsor, died Friday morning.

It can be imagined that the good people of Chester sighed with relief on hearing this news. But their relief was premature. Clarence Adams was yet to make more headlines.

Right from the start he had been a model prisoner. As was only fitting for a library trustee in good standing, he became the prison librarian and developed, so some say, a keen interest in the literature of the occult. He also made friends with a fellow inmate — we don't know his name — who served as the institution's unofficial doctor, or, more likely, as an orderly.

Regulations regarding prison visitors were less severe in those days, and Adams had frequent visits and talks, more or less unsupervised, with William Dunn, his old Chester neighbor. Dunn on his visits to the prison perhaps brought money to Adams. The latter *had* money, for when his estate was probated in 1904, it yielded more than $2,000. And if the part of the story that we are about to relate is true — and as anyone will see, it could be — Adams had need of money. In any case, the former Chester selectman seems to have enjoyed more of the small privileges of prison life than were usually granted to a professional criminal and was on friendly terms with Warden E. W. Oakes, the head of the prison.

Adams's friend, the ubiquitous Mr. Dunn who plays an important role later in our story, remains today something of a mystery man. It was generally thought around town afterwards that Dunn was implicated in the Chester burglaries — it is known that more than one man was involved in at least two of them — but this Adams firmly denied. It may have been this public reflection on his reputation that caused Dunn to move his place of residence several times after leaving Chester: he later lived in Glens Falls, New York, North Springfield, Vermont (where he held town office), in Oklahoma and finally died in Bellows Falls in 1936. One of the many witnesses to this strange story commented years later: "There never was a more likable fellow than Will Dunn." But in the next breath, the informant said he believed him guilty of involvement in the Adams crimes.

It was well into his second winter in the prison, February 22, 1904, to be exact, that Adams, after suffering a bout of rheumatism, was ordered into the prison hospital by Dr. John D. Brewster of Windsor, who also acted as consulting physician to the institution. Here Adams came under the care of his crony, the anonymous inmate orderly. Although nothing seemed very wrong with the prisoner, he began to complain of grippe symptoms; by the next day he was forecasting his own demise.

Adams continued to languish mysteriously on February 24th and 25th. During this time he prepared and had sent to Warden Oakes a testament which requested that in the event of his death his body be prepared by the orderly and be turned over to William Dunn.

On Friday, February 26th, this "doctor" reported to Dr. Brewster that Adams had died. Apparently without examining the deceased, Dr. Brewster signed his death certificate. Cause of death was given as "oedema of the lungs," pneumonia in layman's language. There followed the *Vermont Journal* report we have just quoted.

The detailed events for the next few days, and their sequence, are of great importance to the story.

In spite of the deceased's testament asking that William Dunn be given the body, Warden Oakes telephoned to Clarence Adams's cousin, Samuel Adams, in Chester, asking if the body should be delivered to him. The answer apparently was no.

That Friday afternoon, in accordance with Adams's request, his body was washed by his prison friend, the face shaved and the ears and nostrils stuffed lightly with cotton. The body was dressed in a shroud and was removed to an upstairs room of the prison for the night.

Saturday morning, the 27th, William Dunn appeared at the prison. Whether he came from Glens Falls or Springfield is not

known. Since Warden Oakes had not yet summoned him, it provoked comment at the time, but Dunn explained that Adams, knowing he was dying, had sent for him.

That morning a brief funeral service was held in the prison, and then the coffin was evidently delivered to Dunn and to Lyman Cabot, a local undertaker, at the prison gate. It was taken, apparently that forenoon, directly to Cabot's undertaking establishment in Windsor. There it was placed in a room at the back of the building, whose front portion was a furniture store.

The remains of Clarence Adams rested, for the most part unattended, through Saturday afternoon in the back of the Cabot funeral parlor. Toward evening, according to available evidence, the body in the back room was embalmed by Lyman Cabot, assisted by his nephew, Willard Cabot, of Woodstock in after years. Later in the evening William Dunn, according to contemporary newspaper reports, left for Springfield.

The embalmed body remained in the funeral parlor that night, through Sunday and until Monday morning, when it was taken in a sleigh hearse to Cavendish. Willard Cabot, accompanied by L. C. White of Cavendish drove the hearse via Amsden for the twenty-five miles to the snow-covered village. Henry D. Sanders, the cemetery sexton, took charge of the body at that point, placing it in the customary vault above ground, to await burial when the earth thawed in the Spring.

It would seem that Adams was now finally laid to rest. But no. That April it was noised around that he had been seen in Canada, alive and well. A reputable salesman of Chester, one John Greenwood who worked for Dunham Brothers, the shoe jobber down in Brattleboro, said that he had come face to face with Adams in the lobby of the Hotel Windsor in Montreal. They had recognized each other and had held a conversation. Other reports had it that Clarence Adams was seen later in Nova Scotia, and still later in the West.

By late April of that year the slowly gathering rumors had grown to the proportions of a sensation throughout New England. The metropolitan press, led by the Hearst papers, whipped up the furor.

Some stories implied that between prison and tomb, bricks and stones had been substituted for the body. Cousin Samuel, executor of Clarence's estate, ordered that the body be examined before burial. Samuel himself was coming up to Cavendish to make the identification. But on the day selected, May 1st, a bad storm kept him from making the trip. As a result, Sexton Sanders performed the examination. Cousin Frank Adams also viewed the remains and said it was Clarence. This should have settled the matter. It didn't.

"I thought it looked like Clarence Adams," Sanders was quoted as saying later, "as near as a corpse could that had laid in the tomb two months. I can't say for sure that it was not another body that had been smuggled into the coffin. But one thing I can swear to is that there was a body in the coffin when I buried it, and not a stick of wood and some stones as some folks say."

And the still unidentified body was buried on May Day in the Cavendish Cemetery.

So it is apparent that the truth, or otherwise, of the whole escape episode rests on the word of the traveling salesman, John Greenwood, and possibly other witnesses whose identity is not now known.

It is only fair to observe that the people still alive today who remember the Adams Case of close to seventy years ago are inclined to think of the escape from jail through feigned death as more than doubtful. It is easy, they point out, and perhaps human nature, to ascribe a strange sequel, such as this, to the career of a man who had already won a reputation for the bizarre.

There is little doubt, however, on the basis of what today appears to be solid fact, that Clarence Adams *could* have escaped from prison by feigning death, and have lived out a secret life abroad. The most reasonable arguments in favor of such a thesis would run like this:

1. Adams, a student of the occult, had secretly learned, practiced and perfected self-hypnosis, with the connivance of the prison "doctor." This was the necessary prelude.

2. His lifelong friend William Dunn made sure that the body was left alone in the funeral parlor, and was not yet embalmed for a good part of Saturday afternoon.

3. Lyman Cabot did not view the body, uncovered, until Saturday evening. When he did, he assumed it was Adams's. The body "had a sore on his limb that might be from a shot," Cabot testified in 1905 at an investigation of prison conditions. (But Cabot had never known Adams alive.)

4. Although the great days of body-snatching were long since gone, a cadaver *could* have been smuggled the fifteen miles from the Dartmouth College Medical School in Hanover and switched Saturday afternoon, prior to embalming, by Adams's confederates.

5. Adams, therefore, could have been safely on his way to Canada while the prescribed two and one-half quarts of formaldehyde were being pumped into a nameless corpse from across the Connecticut. The established fact that the embalming was done in Windsor, with a quantity of fluid which would kill any living body, thus nullifies the possibility that Adams escaped en route to Cavendish, or at night was released from the vault. If the body-

switch had failed in Windsor, according to this reasoning, con-federate Dunn would not have allowed the embalming. Then Adams, still in an hypnotic sleep, would have had to chance surviving a twenty-five mile ride in a frigid hearse, and be rescued from the vault in Cavendish.

6. In planning the "death" and escape, why did Adams select the bitter Winter time? Deduction indicates a Summer death in those days would almost immediately have been followed by final burial. Adams understandably did not want to take this chance of being buried alive.

When you come right down to it, no one living today knows whether Clarence Adams, on that fateful February day in 1904, departed this world or merely left Vermont. It is safe to say that every resident of Chester in that bygone era who is alive now, carries his own version, and certainly his own particular memory, of the Adams Case. Just as most of us reading this account can recall what we were doing on Pearl Harbor Day, so various milestones in the curious case of Clarence Adams seem to have left similar, indelible marks on the residents of Chester.

Many still recall with shame the blot on a good town's name. Others remember and grudgingly admire the cleverness of the man. Myron Grimes, who used to drive the stage, stoutly main-tained that Adams was "the smartest man that Chester ever had."

Whether Adams lived or not after 1904, his earlier activities alone mark him as a highly unusual man. He was a kleptomaniac, probably, but hardly a run-of-the-mill specimen, for he seems to have taken considerable pains not to be caught; also he made away with large objects — like the bicycle and the bundles of shingles. Neither the caution nor the size of the booty is typical of kleptomania.

Psychiatrists today probably would pigeonhole Clarence as a psychopathic personality. He could tell right from wrong. He stole in the main not for the value of the objects stolen, but for the sake of taking them. (He must have found a huge secret pleasure by outwitting, time after time, the good burghers of Chester.) And there was undoubtedly an element of compulsion in his actions, although its degree would be difficult to diagnose across the gap of sixty years.

In non-psychiatric terms, if there is a clue to Adams's character it is that he was an incurable romantic who carried into manhood many of the boyhood dreams and perversities that most men outgrow. As he put it himself: "What I have done I attribute to the spirit of adventure that was born in me. I craved some excitement, something to occupy my mind aside from humdrum affairs."

Whatever else Clarence Adams may or may not have done with his life, he never let it be humdrum.

Where Did the Sailor Die?

RALPH NADING HILL

IF THE MESSAGE IN THE MYSTERIOUS LEAD TUBE were true, Samuel Champlain could not have been the first white man to see the Green Mountains. The tube had rolled into a sand pit on the bank of the Missisquoi River a half-mile from Swanton in December 1853, and had been partly filled with a dry substance like gum or putty that had all but disintegrated. Archaic writing on a manuscript inside bore the message:

> *Nov. 29 AD 1564*
> *This is the solme daye*
> *I must now die this is*
> *the 90th day sine we*
> *lef the Ship all have*
> *Perished and on the*
> *Banks of this river*
> *I die to* [or, *so*] *farewelle*
> *may future Posteritye*
> *knowe our end*
> > *Johne Graye*

Orlando Green and P. R. Ripley, who had been digging sand for the marble mills, reported only that the clearly outlined depression where their discovery had lain before it was dislodged into the sand pit, was six inches to a foot below the vegetable mold.

In a dispatch to *The New York Tribune* dated December 6, 1853, a St. Albans correspondent noted that the four-inch tube evidently had been molded in sand around a stick, and the coarse, brownish paper, bearing the message in bold, irregular writing,

33

seemed to resemble that used by the Dutch one-hundred-and-fifty years previously.

Local historians naturally were intrigued. The recorded history of the land that was to become Vermont had always begun with the lucid pages of Champlain's Journal. Here was a document which, if proved authentic, would antedate by over four decades Champlain's July 1609 voyage into the valley that bears his name.

The investigator having most to say about the discovery was the author of the history of Swanton for the *Vermont Historical Magazine*, The Rev. John B. Perry, whom the editor, Abby Hemenway, and Henry Stevens, State Historian, together with the president and professors of the University of Vermont, considered well suited for the task. Perry began his history with the finding of the tube and with the speculation that Johne Graye might have been a member of one of M. Martin Frobisher's sixteenth-century voyages to the New World. Adding ten days to adjust for the discrepancy between the old- and new-style calendars, he calculated that Graye and his companions left their ship on August 31 or September 10, respectively.

While the first recorded voyage of Frobisher to the west in search of an easier route to China took place twelve years later, in 1576, five men indeed became separated from the ship on the coast of Labrador and were never heard from again. The month was August. Ninety days of wandering to the south might easily have brought a survivor to the Missisquoi Valley by late November, the date of Graye's message.

The discrepancy of twelve years could not as logically be accounted for. Still, Richard Hakluyt's version of the Frobisher expedition, printed in 1600, did serve as an indication of the various historic and unrecorded voyages that had taken place by then. Ascending the broad St. Lawrence a number of adventurers like Jacques Cartier, who in 1535 reached the Indian village of Hochelaga (on the later site of lower Montreal), passed within less than seventy miles of the place on the Missisquoi where Graye was presumed to have perished.

In October 1568 a scarcity of food forced the navigator Sir John Hawkins to put a hundred men ashore on the Mexican coast. Most of them perished, but David Ingram survived an eleven-month journey all the way from "Texas" to "Maine" and the St. Johns River. He eventually reached England by way of a French ship, and his adventures were recorded in Hakluyt's folio of 1589. Thirty years passed before a second member of the same expedition was able to return to England. While no record of any northern voyage nearer than Frobisher's to the date of Johne Graye's manuscript appeared to exist, perhaps men lost on the North Atlantic coast in an unrecorded expedition tried to make their way up the Hudson River and Lake Champlain, hoping to reach the St. Lawrence by way of the Richelieu, but instead became lost on the Missisquoi.

Speculation like this was of little value as evidence, but was perhaps useful in making deductions. Among these: It seemed unlikely that a man about to die of exhaustion or cold on a river bank in a bleak forest would have either the inclination to leave a message or the materials to write it with, much less a lead tube or cylinder to preserve it for posterity. The Rev. Mr. Perry nevertheless cited a paragraph from the narrative of the second Frobisher voyage in which the author, Master Dionise Settle, declared that the men who were sent ashore were directed to

leave behind them a letter ["among the Esquimaux"] pen, yncke and paper whereby our men whom the captaine lost the yere before and in that people's custody, might (if any of them were alive), be advertised of our . . . being there.

While little of the foregoing supported the authenticity of the tube, the report of Dr. A. A. Hayes, Assayer of Massachusetts, seemed to Perry quite convincing. Hayes found the substance adhering to the pits in the tube to be carbonate of lead, resulting from its long presence in the sand. The very bright ink on the paper was reported to be galiate or tannate of iron whose appearance, like that of a pigment, was owing to its being dried on an oiled paper. Hayes found the paper

identical with such as is often used by the manufacturers of hardware. It is oiled in the process of manufacture, and for the purpose of increasing its protection of hardware from moisture. . . . It yields to alkali, an oily body appearing like linseed oil. The fibre is of rope, either flax or hemp; it is laid paper well filled.

A waxlike substance on the surface proved to be flour "colored by a pigment, like a wafer. So little is this substance decomposed that it yields starch which gives with iodine water the usual color." Hayes apparently was content to analyze and not to judge. Since the waxlike substance presented obvious proof even to laymen that the paper was not old, investigation ceased. But it was again revived when several reliable witnesses recalled that a "wafer" or transparent seal had been used in fastening the manuscript to the office wall for exhibition (what office Perry did not say). Thus he dismissed the waxlike substance as evidence that the manuscript was not old.

While not claiming to be a graphologist, he noted that the period after the abbreviated form of November was common practice in the sixteenth century, that the absence of other punctuation was not rare, and that there was little unusual about the spelling.

As to the style it is just that which we might naturally look for in a sailor of the period, or perhaps in any one not much used to composing. This is clearly indicated by the short and unconnected sentences, as well as by the redundant expression "future posteritye."

Perry observed that a manuscript with so much "internal evidence" would be difficult to invent, certainly not by its discoverers who testified repeatedly that they were innocent of any fraud. He commented that while

a few are doubtless in some one point competent to perpetrate a literary fraud of this kind, how small is the number of those who would be sufficient to guard against the difficulties in such a variety of points, and to accomplish the whole work in so masterly a way. Had almost anyone undertaken it having considerable skill in such things, he would no doubt have made the doings of Johne Graye synchronize exactly with some known event. . . . Again, few, if any get up . . . a hoax without revealing the secret themselves after a short delay, that they may exhibit their own skill, or make sport of the dupes of their craft.

Perry concluded that while proof of the genuineness of the manuscript was lacking, so was evidence that it was fraudulent. He was inclined to believe it genuine. He had begun his investigation only sixteen years after its discovery. Most of the principals were still alive and no one had volunteered evidence to dispute their claims. Thus the possibility seemed real that Vermont had been visited by men of English extraction before the French.

Here he left the matter. It was occasionally revived during the next nine decades but with little hope of establishing new evidence. In 1949 Earle W. Newton printed a facsimile of the document in his book *The Vermont Story*, stating in the caption: "Extensive researches at the time convinced contemporaries of its authenticity, but the original document has disappeared." Not only the document, as it turned out, but the tube also, thus compounding the mystery! No one in Swanton or Highgate, where the copy, if indeed it was, rested in a vault in the Town Clerk's office, had any knowledge of what had happened to the original.

While preparing a volume on Vermont and New Hampshire during the late 1950's, this writer was tempted to refer to the enigma of the lead tube, but desisted on the following commentary of the recently retired president of the Vermont Historical Society, John P. Clement:

The manuscript in the lead tube . . . seems to me a hoax, like the Indian boy mummy in the Sheldon Museum in Middlebury . . . I've never been able to locate the supposed original or the lead tube. But I did find the paper that is sometimes claimed to be the original in the Highgate Library.

I sent this to the Huntington Library in California which pronounced the paper to be of 19th-century origin, the ink to be of mid-19th century, and the process to have been lithography. I also sent it to Dr. Samuel Eliot Morison at Harvard, who said the script was impossible for the 16th century, and the spelling equally phony. He called it a hoax.

These judgments seemed about as final as reliable authorities could pronounce.

There remained, however, the question of what happened to the tube and the original manuscript analyzed by the assayer of Massachusetts. If the Huntington Library and Dr. Morison had examined a facsimile, their report of the ink and paper was of no value. If the script and spelling were fraudulent it of course did not matter whether the document was an original or a copy. Even if it were a hoax, like the Cardiff Giant, its mysterious origin had still to be explained.

In 1961 Mr. E. J. Tyler, partner in the Swanton law firm of Webster and Tyler, inquired of the history department of the University of Vermont whether a "carbon-dating" process might determine the age of the Graye document. The reason it was now in Highgate, he explained, was that a Dr. Baxter had apparently purchased it and brought it there from Swanton. It had been given to the Highgate library where it was examined by many people. Indeed, it was Tyler's impression that it had been lent out on a few occasions. He thought it looked "suspiciously well preserved for a paper that even purports to be almost four hundred years old."

T. D. Seymour Bassett, Curator of the Wilbur Collection of the University of Vermont wrote, among others, Alfred F. Whiting, Curator of Anthropology, Dartmouth College Museum, who replied that while carbon-dating had improved in recent years, trying to establish a date of three-hundred years ago with a probable error of one-hundred-and-fifty years seemed to him scarcely worthwhile. A study of the script might be more rewarding, and Bassett (who was not aware of the report to John P. Clement of Samuel Eliot Morison and the Huntington Library in California wrote Tyler that he was referring the facsimile to some of the University's English scholars for comment. They reported that they did not think there was anything wrong with the spelling, which varied greatly, although one professor was inclined to suspect "solme" because most of the sixteenth-century samples previously encountered had been spelled "solempne," or some similar variation with a *p*. Judgment was difficult without the original document but they offered to seek the help of experts in Renaissance language.

Tyler did not pursue the correspondence nor Bassett his inquiries. The thread was picked up in 1964 by Walter Hard, Jr., editor of *Vermont Life*, who started an independent investigation that might produce revelations of interest to readers of the magazine. One of the scholars to whom he wrote was Alan Cooke of the Scott Polar Research Institute, Cambridge, England, in the hope of obtaining further research on the Frobisher and other early expeditions to America. Cooke was glad to help, particularly since he had been born in Montpelier and raised on a farm in Waitsfield. On June 8, 1965, Cooke was able to report that after

casting about in such books and archives as seemed obvious in search of a 1564 voyage to which your document might bear some relation, and having found none, I wrote to Professor David B. Quinn (Modern History, University of Liverpool), whose work is probably familiar to you. He has edited a number of Hakluyt volumes and is the generally acknowledged authority on early English voyages to North America. On February 16 he wrote me: "The hand is rather one of the eighteenth century. If it is not an eighteenth century fake it is a modern one attempting to use an old hand but not a sufficiently antique one." He later showed the photocopy, which I had lent to him, to Dr. Oschinsky, lecturer in Palaeography, and on June 3 further commented, " . . . our opinion is that it cannot be earlier than nineteenth century and could be more recent." He reads line 8 "so Farewelle," and thinks the signature is probably "Johne Gedge."

These things are, of course, matters of informed opinion. It may be possible to find someone of competent judgment who inclines to view the document more favorably. But I do not think there can be many such who would care to gainsay Professor Quinn. Moreover, there appears to be no record of a voyage about that date to which the document might be attached. Rather a disappointment, I know. Even if it be a fake, it has a certain interest of its own.

Unless the original document somehow is found, it seems unlikely that anyone will produce further evidence in the strange case of John Graye — too strange, it appears, to be true. Yet responsible new claims of voyages earlier than that of Columbus to the New World enhance the possibility that there were white men in Vermont even earlier than 1564 — the date that the mysterious lead tube will not let us quite forget.

Fall of the House of Hayden

LOUIS A. LAMOUREUX

THE MELLOWED BRICK of the great mansion glowed in the light of the Autumn sun that October afternoon in 1910 as the black hearse grated along the South Albany Road, not far from the Canadian border, bearing to the village churchyard the remains of William Henry Hayden, last in the male line of his family. Heavy brocaded curtains, faded and dusty, were drawn across the mansion windows, as they had been these past eighteen years that the richly furnished house had lain untenanted.

Some among the funeral party remembered Mercie Dale's curse — that the Hayden name would perish. How certain it seemed now of fulfillment! Others, passing by the mansion at dusk, looked uneasily toward the darkened house and its three imposing barns. What would happen to it now? Where lay the Hayden fortune?

But Henry Hayden had carried many secrets with him to his grave.

Nothing like the Hayden Mansion has been built in these parts before or since. They chose for the site a broad intervale in the Black River Valley. The mansion, in contrast to the modest wooden dwellings of the area, was a Victorian version of the Colonial style. Although restrained in design, its excellent proportions even today convey elegance. This was what Henry's father was after when, a decade before the Civil War, he set out to show what money could do.

Brick for the walls was kilned on a farm across the Black River, and only this of the house seems native to the region. Originally there was a two-and-a-half story brick ell, half the length of the main house. Attached to it was another ell of wood a story-and-a-half in height, and used as servants' quarters. Plans for

41

formal Italianate gardens were never developed, although a large pool was formed when fill was excavated south of the house to grade the front lawn. Behind were three enormous barns.

The interior of the mansion is still remembered by many both for its architectural features and sumptuous furnishings. Through the paneled front door one entered a fair-sized front hall with a short graceful staircase, its fretwork balusters curving to a second floor. A glass, urnlike ornament called a "wishing well" was mounted on the newel post. Rooms had high ceilings with molded plaster cornices and recessed windows with paneling. The more formal rooms had elaborate chandeliers with engraved glass globes and crystal pendants.

The decoration and furnishings were luxurious. Contrasting

with the white of the heavy paneled doors and the ceilings, were the deep, dark colors of velvet or brocaded window draperies, suspended from ornate, gilded cornices and piling generously in folds on the thick Persian rugs. Crystal ware and silver in every conceivable form, highly polished tables, plump upholstered chairs, grand pianos and dazzling linen, remained in the minds of visitors.

There was a long dining room at the back of the house with a table which would seat thirty. There was a small bridal chamber with canopied four-poster, and a sickroom fitted with all the conveniences of the day. What seemed to most the height of opulence was the ballroom on the third floor of the main house. It had a vaulted, plaster ceiling, benches all round, a stage for the orchestra and, above all, a spring floor.

For all its many chimneys — four in the main house — the mansion had no fireplaces. In the cellar was an early and gargan-tuan hot-air furnace so big it would take six-foot logs. What appeared to be fireplaces on the inside walls actually were furnace registers with grilled openings framed by mantels of cast metal painted to resemble dark marble.

But no fine mansion awaited the first William Hayden, Henry's grandfather, when he with his wife, Silence, and her mother, Mercie Dale, first arrived in Albany, then known as Lutterloh.

The Haydens, married in 1798, had journeyed from Braintree, Massachusetts, by ox cart over the Hazen Military Road, and for the first few years had pioneered in neighboring Craftsbury. Widow Mercie Dale was well-to-do for that day and helped the young couple over the rough times. In 1806 William bought Lot Number 4 in Lutterloh, and soon moved from their rude cabin to a frame house.

His few fellow townsmen found William a shrewd and ambi-tious man. He was named highway surveyor when the town was organized, and took his pay in extra land. During the next few years he served as a selectman, was elected captain of the first militia, kept the first public house, and then started a spinning and weaving mill which employed several women. He was the area's first and only customs officer — until the rise of cattle smuggling in his area lost him the appointment.

Through the years William had been acquiring so much land

that by 1823 he was overextended and in serious financial straits. Although Mercie had advanced money to her son-in-law in earlier years, he apparently never repaid it and kept nagging her for more. Embittered and suspicious, Mercie fell into a long illness. Finally she came to accuse William of poisoning her.

Then one day, near the end and in the presence of Silence, she pronounced her famous curse: "The Hayden name shall die in the third generation, and the last to bear the name shall die in poverty."

In her final days Mercie was cared for by a neighbor Sally Rogers, and when she died (the date unknown) she had made certain of burial in the Rogers family cemetery, disdaining to share the same ground with the Haydens.

William's troubles all seem to have come to a head by 1830, although they had been brewing for the better part of a decade. He and Silence, by one account, had raised five sons and four daughters by then, but census records indicate only a twin son and daughter living to majority.

Numerous lawsuits finally lost William everything. William, Jr., now thirty years of age, was his codefendant in some, but himself had at least four writs later issued against his father — for recovery of a black horse (value of $40), of a lost gold watch (found by his father but not returned), and for loans never repaid.

To escape these bitter family quarrels and his creditors, William finally decamped to Potton, Quebec, just across the border. It appears that Silence and two young sons went with him.

He lived in Potton until 1838 and then, involved in the Papineau Rebellion, was forced to flee back across the border to North Troy. Family tradition said William's Canadian trouble stemmed from his declaiming — even though Victoria then was reigning — "To Hell with the King." Whatever the cause, William was decoyed back into Canada, but escaped in the woods while being taken to the Montreal jail. He emigrated to the "West," never returning to Albany, and died at Farnshoile, New York, in 1846.

Whether Silence lived with her husband in exile from Vermont is not known — neither is it certain whether one or both of the young sons survived. There is no indication that she ever again lived in Albany, although she must have kept in touch with her Vermont son in his later days of wealth. For when Silence died (we do not know where) in 1872 at the age of ninety-four, and when the news reached Albany, William, Jr., ordered the village church bell tolled.

In the second generation we have record of only two living to maturity. Arathuza died at sixty-four in Albany, apparently a spinster. Her twin, young William, remained to carry on the Hayden name.

But William, Jr., or Will as he was called, was emerging as a "comer" by the time his father decamped. He was married to Azubah Culver of Albany, and by her had five children (one son) who reached maturity.

Will was both a farmer and a cooper, until he decided to try a railroad-building contract in New Hampshire. In this he prospered, later extending his work as far as Michigan and into Canada. He was absent from Albany in these pursuits for many years on end, building in all 586 miles of line and amassing a considerable fortune.

We don't know when Will Hayden conceived of his mansion, but it is quite certain his motive was to build a monument to himself. Owning a fine horse and rig was the status symbol of that day, but Will had different ideas. "I'll show those damned fools in Albany what money can do." And he proceeded to.

Tradition says that Will's elder daughter was married in the new mansion's ballroom in 1843, but old family account books, listing purchase of great quantities of brick and window weights, for instance, suggest it wasn't started until 1854. A workman's signature date, still to be found in the old plaster, confirms this.

Will never quite finished off the mansion as he'd planned. Ornamental ironwork never graced the granite curbings, and one room was never used; nor had he made his planned visit to England and to select its furnishing. For already the shadows of Mercie Dale's curse were falling. There was family illness and instability among his children, the later estrangement with wife, Azubah, and his own failing sight.

Meanwhile the Haydens in the new mansion had taken up a mode of life that was the wonder of the region. Azubah and daughter Julia would be taken for pleasure drives in one of the handsome carriages drawn by blooded horses. There were two servants, and on New Year's Eve a great party would be held in the third-floor ballroom.

Will obviously relished being the country squire, but railroad work continued to take him away for long periods. More money was needed to maintain this style of living.

There were nine-hundred acres with the mansion and four-hundred more with the old Hayden farm near by, and it always pleased Will to be asked how much land he owned. "All that you can see," he would reply with pride.

He favored old clothes, and when about the farm usually wore the old farmer's long blue smock, wide-brimmed hat and boots. The story is told of a day when he was returning from a sheep pasture on foot, looking his worst, and a passing Newport minister offered a lift in his buggy. Noting Will's poor apparel the minister asked to send Will a pair of his old trousers. Will allowed that he could use them. As the horse trotted up to the mansion driveway, Will told his benefactor to drive in. The minister asked if he worked there. "I own the place," Will admitted, and, it being close to dinner time, he gave orders for "the best meal you can prepare." As the dazed clergyman was driving away later, Will called after him: "Don't forget the pants."

In spite of the mansion's elegance and lavish furnishings there is no evidence the Haydens were strong for education or acquired any degree of culture. Nor did they seek to achieve any social or civic distinctions. Although they were Spiritualists they supported the local Congregational church. Except for Hemenway's *Gazetteer* neither Will nor the other members of the family ever were mentioned in the several biographical compendiums of the century. Of Will Miss Hemenway wrote in 1870: "His history as a railroad contractor, both in the States and Canada, has never been tarnished by any act of malice or injustice to those who have labored for him." Equivocally the item ends: "Even now the essence of human kindness must be drawn from him, but it cannot be done with a blister."

For a while the family's life seemed normal enough, and perhaps Mercie Dale's curse was almost forgotten. Will and Azubah's daughters were all married and presenting grandchildren regularly. It is true that the one son, William Henry (known as Henry) had

always seemed erratic and undependable, but he had married
Lydia Crosby of Waterville, Maine, was living on the old home-
place, and had started a family of his own.

Soon, however, things began to worsen. Will arrived home
after one of his long absences on business in 1862. His trusted
farm manager was found somewhat later badly beaten. The cause
of the dispute, now uncertain, apparently involved Will's jealousy
of the attentions that the manager was paying to Azubah. The
man's name is lost to history, but it appears somewhere among
the roster of sixteen Albany men who enlisted for the Union cause
in 1862. From this time forward there was a lifelong estrangement

between Will and Azubah. They continued to follow the genteel life at the mansion, but communicated with each other only through a third party — Henry or a servant. But Will remained, by report, unfailingly courteous to others, and Azubah "was considered the gracious lady by all who knew her."

One tragedy then followed another. Will and Azubah's married daughter, Mary, sickened soon after she had lost her fourth child, and herself went insane and died. Four years later Will's only Hayden grandson, William Andrew, died at the age of five; his daughter Julia was the next to go.

By now Will's eyesight was failing, and when in 1883 he was stricken with apoplexy, he was almost totally blind. Azubah, his widow, lived out her days in the already declining mansion to the age of eighty-three. The large farm, apparently, never itself supported the family's style of living, for an inventory of Will's estate after his death placed its total value at $19,551.53.

On Christmas Day of 1891, about a month before she died, Azubah made out her will. It bequeathed the apparently modest estate left to her by one Lavinia Fuller (perhaps a relative on her mother's side) to the wife of son William Henry, to Henry's two living daughters and to Julia's two daughters — but not a penny to Henry himself. Earlier that year Henry had tried to get title to sell Will and Azubah's real estate, and this may have so displeased his mother that she cut him off. Meanwhile, there still was no settlement of the estate of Will Hayden, who had died in 1883.

Henry, who from boyhood seems to have been the black sheep of the family, was hearty of manner, a rawboned six-footer who "looked like Uncle Sam." Henry maintained the appearances of a prosperous farmer, although not equal to the style of his parents. He kept a fine herd of registered Jerseys and raced his blooded horses at nearby fairs.

People were suspicious of Henry. He lived on the farm-place but secured the mansion key when his mother died. Just before Azubah's funeral a servant, as she recounted later, observed him in the mansion taking papers from a safe and burning them. "There, by God, we'll see," he muttered.

Had Henry fixed the inheritance in his own favor? At any rate a great and protracted family squabble broke out after Azubah's burial. It is quite possible that Henry and his brother-in-law Bill Blaisdell were in cahoots. Both entered large claims against Will's estate, and neither contested the other's claim. But the McClary and Dow relatives called them "wholly fraudulent" and fought these moves bitterly.

In spite of their opposition, Henry remained as administrator of the unsettled estate for twenty-seven years — until his own death. And after that Bill Blaisdell kept the litigation going.

Finally, in 1915 Blaisdell talked Henry's daughter, Mamie, into signing a bad bargain. He got $8,500 from the estate and she and Julia Ella Blaisdell were to get the rest. But this remainder, it turned out, was entirely in the form of a court judgment (for $40,496.80) issued against one H. E. Fuller way back in 1874. It is doubtful that Mamie or Julia Ella ever received a cent of this old claim, which was not even listed in Will's estate inventory of 1883.

As it turned out, Blaisdell finally received $7,500 when Will's estate was closed, but Mamie received nothing — nor did anyone else. Some did go to Henry's estate, however, and here is what of the Hayden fortunes finally came in 1915 to Mamie:

Household Furniture	$395.00
Buggy	20.00
Cash	977.51
	$1,392.51

And so the mansion remained closed as the litigation and the years stretched onward. There were strange happenings, though — rumors of moving lights inside late at night; sometimes the sounds, carrying to the road, of heavy movement inside the house. Some, remembering the seances of years ago, laid it to ghosts of the departed Haydens. One man to this day maintained he once heard an orchestra playing in the dark and abandoned ballroom.

Others believe these nocturnal mysteries were related to the smuggling of Chinese, a profitable activity (also linked to Henry) until after the Boxer Rebellion, when Chinese then could enter this country legally. Some say more than one Chinese lies buried in the apple orchard behind the mansion. At any rate, there were tunnels at one time running from the cellar of the house to the barn. A post-Hayden owner, probably fearing someone might be trapped, years later filled them in.

For many years after Azubah's death the house remained closed and mysterious, and the few who had occasion to go inside found it a chilling experience — hushed and dark, white dust protectors covering the furniture. So airtight was the house — possibly that was the cause — that when you opened one door, others would slam heavily in the distant darkness.

What happened to the rest of the family fortune? Some think that Henry knew. He always told his daughter Armenia Mamie she would be well fixed financially when he died. And when that day came in 1910, Henry, stricken with a cerebral hemorrhage, lay on his deathbed desperately but vainly trying to tell Mamie something — perhaps where Will and Azubah's fortune (which some felt he had looted) was concealed.

By the time the estates at last were settled (after Henry had gone silent to his grave) most of the legatees themselves had died. For dark and melancholy-appearing Mamie, last of the Haydens, there was virtually nothing. Gone now were all the rest — her little brother years ago, her twin in 1891, and sister Carrie taken the same year as her father.

Mamie, the frail and shy, the last known to bear the Hayden name, went back to her mother's old home in Maine. There in 1927, poverty stricken and alone, she died.

In 1913 the mansion and all its furnishings were sold — for $8,300.

The money probably went into Will's unsettled estate. The new owner, during the eight years he lived there, sold off the mansion's contents "at a handsome profit," and then, doing better than anyone had since Will Hayden's heyday, he sold the bare place and land to a Canadian family for $25,000.

Those who remember these things say that the mansion now entered on a new career — extensive bootlegging. The new owners were a sociable lot and held public dances in the old ballroom. The tunnels, useful in the "Chinese era," probably came in handy again for this fresh, clandestine trade.

The Canadians sold out in 1922, and from then on the Hayden Mansion went downhill fast, each successive owner finding that hard times had replaced elegant living. Land was sold off piecemeal, barns burned, the house fell into disrepair, and finally fire destroyed the brick ell.

After that the place was abandoned, and for many years it was open, inside and out, to passing vandals. Only now is its future bright again. The house and seven acres were acquired around 1957 by Mr. and Mrs. William Chadwick, formerly of Texas, who are gradually restoring the property. To date more than seven thousand bricks from the ruined ell have been cleaned, also, preparatory to rebuilding it.

But for the Haydens, all is past. Their fortune vanished with the family name. Its secret lies somewhere among the graves at the head of Albany Cemetery. Here the Haydens are ranged in front. Squarely behind lie the Blaisdells, uniform marble head- and foot-stones giving an illusion of family unity.

Of them all, Mercie Dale in her lost grave, can rest in peace now. Her curse has been fulfilled.

The Deep Frozen Folk of Farmer Morse

WESLEY S. GRISWOLD

PERHAPS NO FANTASTIC YARN idly spun in Vermont has ever won a wider audience, or taken longer doing it, than "A Strange Tale," which first appeared on the front page of the Montpelier *Argus and Patriot*, then a popular weekly newspaper, on December 21, 1887.

The story, purporting to be true, was a morbid and gripping one with a Poe-like flavor. It told of a family of wretchedly poor settlers in the northern part of the state who had established the practice of putting their oldest and least able relatives into cold storage each Winter, thawing them out in time to help with Spring planting.

"I am an old man," began the teller of this weird tale, then identified only by the initials *A. M.*, "and have seen some strange sights in the course of a roving life in foreign lands as well as in this country, but none so strange as one found recorded in an old diary, kept by my Uncle William, that came into my possession a few years ago, at his decease."

Here was a tempting beginning, the mark of a seasoned spinner of yarns, and the author skillfully proceeded to strengthen the impression that he was telling the truth.

"The events described took place in a mountain town some twenty miles from Montpelier, the capital of Vermont," he continued. "I have been to the place on the mountain, and seen the old log house where the events I found recorded in the diary took place, and seen and talked with an old man who vouched for the truth of the story, and that his father was one of the parties operated on. The account runs in this wise:"

53

January 7: I went on the mountain today, and witnessed what to me was a horrible sight. It seems that the dwellers there who are unable, either from age or other reasons, to contribute to the support of their families, are disposed of in the Winter months in a manner that will shock the one who reads this diary, unless that person lives in that vicinity. I will describe what I saw. Six persons, four men and two women, one of the men a cripple about thirty-years-old, the other five past the age of usefulness, lay on the earthy floor of the cabin drugged into insensibility, while members of their families were gathered about them in apparent indifference. In a short time the unconscious bodies were inspected by several old people, who said, "They are ready." They were then stripped of all their clothing, except a single garment. Then the bodies were carried outside, and laid on logs exposed to the bitter cold mountain air, the operation having been delayed several days for suitable weather.

It was night when the bodies were carried out, and the full moon, occasionally obscured by flying clouds, shone on their upturned ghastly faces, and a horrible fascination kept me by the bodies as long as I could endure the severe cold. Soon the noses, ears and fingers began to turn white, then the limbs and face assumed a tallowy look. I could stand the cold no longer, and went inside, where I found the friends in cheerful conversation.

In about an hour I went out and looked at the bodies; they were fast freezing. Again I went inside, where the men were smoking their clay pipes, but silence had fallen on them; perhaps they were thinking of the time when their turn would come to be cared for in the same way. One by one they at last lay down on the floor and went to sleep. It seemed a horrible nightmare to me, and I could not think of sleep. I could not shut out the sight of those freezing bodies outside, neither could I bear to be in darkness, but I piled on the wood in the cavernous fireplace, and, seated on a shingle block, passed the dreary night, terror-stricken by the horrible sights I had witnessed.

January 8: Day came at length, but did not dissipate the terror that filled me. The frozen bodies became visible, white as the snow that lay in huge drifts about them. The women gathered about the fire and soon commenced preparing breakfast. The men awoke and, conversation again commencing, affairs assumed a more cheerful aspect. After breakfast the men lighted their pipes, and some of them took a yoke of oxen and went off toward the forest, while others proceeded to nail together boards, making a box about ten feet long and half as high and wide. When this was completed they placed about two feet of straw in the bottom; then they laid three of the frozen bodies on the straw. Then the faces and upper part of the bodies were covered with a cloth, then more straw was put in the box, and the other three bodies placed on top and covered the same as the first ones, with cloth and straw. Boards were then firmly nailed on the top, to protect the bodies from being injured by carnivorous animals that make their home on these mountains.

By this time the men who went off with the ox-team returned with a huge load of spruce and hemlock boughs, which they unloaded at the foot of a steep ledge; came to the house and loaded the box containing the bodies on the sled, and drew it to the foot of the ledge, near the load of boughs. These were soon piled on and around the box, and it was left to be covered with snow, which I was told would lie in drifts twenty feet deep over this rude tomb. "We shall want our men to plant our corn next spring," said a youngish-looking woman, the wife of one of the frozen men, "and if you want to see them resuscitated you come here about the 10th of next May."

With this agreement I left the mountaineers, living and frozen, to their fate, and returned to my home in Boston, where it was weeks before I was fairly myself, as my thoughts would return to that mountain with its awful sepulchre.

"Turning the leaves of the old diary to the date of May 10, the following entry was found:"

May 10: I arrived here at 10 A.M., after riding about four hours over muddy, unsettled roads. The weather is warm and pleasant, most of the snow is gone, except here and there drifts in the fence corners and hollows, but nature is not yet dressed in green. I found the same parties here that I left last January, ready to disinter the bodies of their friends. I had no expectations of finding any life there, but a feeling that I could not resist impelled me to come and see. We repaired at once to the well-remembered spot at the ledge. The snow had melted from the top of the brush, but still lay deep around the bottom of the pile. The men commenced work at once, some shoveling away the snow and others tearing away the brush. Soon the box was visible. The cover was taken off, the layers of straw removed, and the bodies, frozen and apparently lifeless, lifted out and laid on the snow. Large troughs made out of hemlock logs were placed near by, filled with tepid water, into which the bodies were separately placed, with the head slightly raised. Boiling water was then poured into the trough from kettles hung on poles near

by, until the water in the trough was as hot as I could hold my hand in. Hemlock boughs had been put in the boiling water in such quantities that they had given the water the color of wine. After lying in this bath about an hour, color began to return to the bodies, when all hands began rubbing and chafing them. This continued about another hour, when a slight twitching of the muscles of the face and limbs, followed by audible gasps, showed that life was not quenched, and that vitality was returning. Spirits were then given in small quantities, and allowed to trickle down their throats. Soon they could swallow, and more was given them, when their eyes opened, and they began to talk, and finally sat up in their bathtubs. They were then taken out and assisted to the house, where after a hearty dinner they seemed as well as ever, and in nowise injured, but rather refreshed, by their long sleep of four months.

Truly, truth is stranger than fiction.

There the story ended, but not its career, which proved to be very late-blooming.

The six thousand subscribers to the *Argus and Patriot* ("much the largest circulation of any Vermont newspaper," it boasted) could scarcely have failed to be fascinated by this gruesome tale, though none of them was sufficiently moved by it to write a letter to the editor questioning, condemning, or confirming it. At least, if any letters were received, the editor chose not to publish them. Quite possibly most readers of the *Argus and Patriot* had been persuaded that despite the story's vividness and trappings of apparent truth, it was really fiction. There were at least three good reasons for thinking so: *A. M.* had not identified the mountain town where the deep-freezing of these human beings had occurred, though he had said it was only twenty miles from Montpelier; he had not specified the year when his uncle's diary entries were written; and he had not, after all, identified himself.

The tall tale might have been forgotten forever if Hannah F. Stevens of Bridgewater, an inveterate cutter of clippings that interested her, hadn't pasted the *Argus and Patriot* story in her scrapbook — neglecting, however, to note where it came from or when it was printed. The yarn was suddenly revived fifty-two years later, when Hannah's by then elderly son discovered the scrapbook among his mother's effects and called the attention of a Rutland newspaperman to "A Strange Tale."

On May 24, 1939, the Rutland *Herald* reprinted *A. M.*'s story, word for word, explaining that no one knew its source. Four days later, the Boston *Globe* picked it up, and it was well launched into New England folklore. In April 1940, *Yankee Magazine* published an account of the story — and later republished it in response to popular request. The *Old Farmer's Almanac* of 1943 gave "A Strange Tale" further publicity. So did Alton Hall Blackington, who told *A. M.*'s story on the radio and in lectures, and Charles Edward Crane, who included it in his book *Winter in Vermont*. The yarn, in fact, won vastly increased circulation, but it remained entirely a mystery until 1949. Even then, only part of its origin was uncovered.

In the 1949–50 Fall–Winter issue of *Vermont Life*, Roland W. Robbins, a writer and lecturer on aspects of rural New England, reported that with the aid of the Vermont State Library he had tracked "A Strange Tale" to its original publication in the *Argus and Patroit*. He was still baffled, though, by the identity of its author, and invited his readers to help in identifying him.

It was not until two years later, however, that Robbins was able at last to expose the man hiding behind the initials *A. M.* as having been Allen Morse, a decidedly untypical dairy farmer of Calais, just north of Montpelier, who was born in 1835 and died in 1917. Morse's granddaughter, Mrs. Mabel E. Hynes of Agawam, Massachusetts, made the revelation, after having belatedly been told about Robbins's article on "A Strange Tale." She sent Robbins a snapshot of her maternal grandfather that had been taken in his later years, and a brief account of the genesis of his story of the aged and crippled mountaineers who, for economy's sake, had been regularly frozen for the winter.

The snapshot of Allen Morse showed a pleasant-looking old gentleman of broad, calm features and stocky body, tilted back comfortably in a rocking chair on his lawn and reading a newspaper. His gray hair was neatly cut and brushed, his full beard cropped close to his cheeks and chin. His vest was unbuttoned from the bottom to the halfway point to ease a well-fed stomach; his feet were in carpet slippers. It was late afternoon, for the shadows were long on the grass behind his chair. Farmer Morse was the picture of genial contentment, and didn't look in the least capable of concocting horror stories.

Yet Mrs. Hynes remembered that Morse had had a deep interest in spiritualism, had told with relish of his own encounters with the supernatural, and she had heard him tell "A Strange Tale" many times in her youth. He had first frightened her with it when she was ten years old, though he quickly routed her fears with amusing stories about his imaginary young Indian friends. He was the best storyteller in a family whose chief entertainment at its annual reunions was "yarnin'," as they called their competitive efforts to tell tall tales.

"A Strange Tale," further embellished with each successive tell-ing, became so familiar to the Morses and their in-laws and cousins, said Mrs. Hynes, that it was indulgently called "Grandpa's yarn." Mrs. Hynes recalled that Allen Morse first tried it out on the family audience at an August picnic at the end of haying, and that it had topped a lurid account by his brother-in-law, William Noyes, of having seen bright flames dancing above a fresh grave as he passed a cemetery on his way to the picnic. Noyes, by the way, was known to the entire family as "Uncle William," and Mrs. Hynes felt certain that it was he whom Grandpa Morse had had in mind as the fictitious diarist of "A Strange Tale."

Allen Morse used his literary talents in more practical ways, too. For several years, Mrs. Hynes reported, he wrote articles on both agricultural and political topics for various periodicals, con-tributed stories to the *New England Homestead*, and occasionally wrote verse. He did not commit "A Strange Tale" to paper, however, until urged to do so by his eldest daughter, Mrs. Hynes's mother, who in 1887 was working for the Montpelier *Argus and Patriot* as a typesetter and proofreader. When she had succeeded in persuading her father to write out "Grandpa's yarn," gracing it with all his favorite inventions, she secretly arranged with her boss, the editor of the newspaper, to publish "A Strange Tale" on Morse's next birthday, December 21, 1887.

The author was delighted when his daughter's surprise was delivered, though undoubtedly relieved that she had kept his identity a mystery. To have signed his name to the eerie story, as his daughter was well aware, would have been to label it immediately, for all who knew him, as purely a product of his fertile imagination and would have ruined the effect of the yarn at the start. The opening of the very first sentence would have given him away: "I am an old man [he was only fifty-two years old the day the story was printed] and have seen some strange sights in the course of a roving life in foreign lands as well as in this country [he had lived on a farm in Calais since he was a small child] . . . "

So much for the unmasking of the mythmaker. What Mrs. Hynes hadn't explained was that the setting and the period of Allen Morse's earlier years had contributed importantly to his becoming a spinner of morbid yarns. Calais was then a tiny community on the fringe of wilderness, the largely uninhabited region of the Worcester Mountains. Life there was hard and death came early, often in epidemics that swept through the countryside undeterred by the feeble remedies of primitive doctors. More than once while Morse was growing up, epidemics of typhoid and diphtheria carried off friends and neighbors of his. When they died in Winter, their bodies had to be kept more or less as those in "A Strange Tale" were preserved, until the ground became soft enough in the Spring to bury them. This familiar fact may well have provided the inspiration for Morse's favorite yarn.

The region was also highly receptive to fantasy, and rich in quirky characters. When Allen was a child of eight, the Millerite religious contagion was at its height, and it had a firm grip on Calais. William Miller's followers — said to have reached the astonishing total of fifty thousand or more throughout New England and New York State — devoutly believed his prediction that the world was going to come to an end at midnight on December 31, 1843, with sea and land yielding up their dead and the faithful ascending to Heaven. An exceptionally dazzling display of falling stars ten years earlier when the earth was passing through the region of the Leonids in November, as it always does, and the sudden, blazing appearance of Halley's Comet in 1834, had lent wings to Miller's apocalyptic prophecies, and had a profoundly sobering effect on a gullible public almost wholly ignorant of scientific truths.

Young Allen Morse was probably not among the crowd that crammed into the Old West Church, most familiar landmark in Calais Town, on the last night of 1843 — but nearly everyone else in the community was there, believer and scoffer alike. A grandfather's clock was set up beside the pulpit, and when it began striking the hour of midnight, some women screamed, others fainted, and mass ascension of the faithful, as Miller had promised, seemed very near. When ten minutes passed, however, without yawning of graves in the churchyard or skyward flights by the better-behaved members of the congregation, the tide of Millerism abruptly ran out in Calais.

The town still retained more than its fair share of eccentrics, though, including Allen Morse's neighbor Pardon Janes, whose strange career is discussed elsewhere in this book.

Given an intellectual climate and human oddities such as Calais provided, and a period in our social history when swapping stories was a highly acceptable form of communal entertainment, is it any wonder that a born storyteller like Allen Morse should have concocted "A Strange Tale"?

Not many years after the first appearance of Morse's macabre yarn, the highly respected journal *Scientific American* printed a pathetic story of human pseudo-hibernation in Russia, an account gleaned from an official report made by the Bureau of Statistics of the Department of Pskov. The report, summarized by *Scientific American* in its issue of January 20, 1900, told of peasants who, when food supplies were inadequate for their normal needs during a Winter (which was usually the case), deliberately conditioned themselves to sleeping the four or five months away. They would get up only often enough to keep a fire going and occasionally eat a piece of black bread dipped in water. The rest of the time, said the report, they lay on top of their flat stoves or in the warmest corners of their huts in a state of almost complete immobility, and got through the Winter with a minimal expenditure of energy and the scantiest consumption of food. *Lejka*, as the Russians called this pitiful practice, resembled the state of suspended animation achieved by animal hibernators. It was far removed, however, from the wholly lifeless wintering of Allen Morse's fictitious folk, who were frozen to death and resurrected when convenient. This, despite impressive accomplishments in recent years by medical and biological scientists in the beneficial uses of low temperatures, still remains a technical impossibility.

True, doctors do routinely induce brief periods of artificial hibernation, which they call hypothermia, for delicate heart or brain surgery. Partly by icy baths, they lower the patient's body temperature abnormally in order to slow his metabolism and reduce his brain's need for oxygen during the operation. To avoid the necessity of the frigid baths, Soviet scientists have recently devised a small electric refrigerator in the shape of a helmet, which, they claim, will cool the brain of the wearer to 72° in a couple of minutes. This leads to a drastic reduction in his body temperature for the ensuing surgery.

Individuals have safely endured body temperatures as low as 36° for the better part of an hour. One young Cuban stowaway even managed somehow to survive a nine-hour flight in the wheel-well of a transatlantic jet while outside temperatures dropped to 40° below zero and his oxygen supply, at an altitude of 30,000 feet, became essentially nil. Doctors were astounded that he lived to tell about his incredible experience.

Cornea, skin, bone-marrow cells, sperm, and red blood-cells survive freezing and thawing without apparent harm, but whole human beings are quite a different matter. Science at its present level of sophistication declares that when ice crystals have formed in as much as 50 percent of the body water of any higher animal, and especially man, that creature has gone beyond recall.

Still, hope persists in some quarters that situations such as Allen Morse invented more than eighty years ago are within the realm of future possibility, if not in the grasp of the present.

Groups calling themselves Cryonics Societies have formed in New York, Michigan, California, and elsewhere. Members of these societies believe so eagerly in the eventual feasibility of resurrecting frozen human beings at will that several, now dead, arranged before their demise to have themselves entombed in metal capsules chilled to $-321°F$ by liquid nitrogen. There they will remain until that expected day when, they trust, science will have learned how to revive them, in response to their written requests, and cure whatever ailment killed them.

Grandpa Morse would doubtless have been fascinated to hear about *that*.

The Sad Fate of John O'Neil

GEORGE G. CONNELLY

VERMONT HORSE-RACING IS A MIXED BLESSING to Massachusetts. Neighboring Green Mountain Park furnishes an exciting pastime, but the traffic is an expensive menace. Vermont liquor, on the contrary, is a delightful bargain to nearby residents of New York and Massachusetts.

It has not always been this way, for Vermont like Maine used to be bone dry, with most of its cheer coming by dark of night from wicked New Yorkers. This so disturbed the W.C.T.U. that they finally decided to take action.

The day after Christmas 1882, J. P. Cain, a grand juror of Rutland, made a written complaint to Justice of the Peace Wayne Bailey, that John O'Neil of Whitehall, New York, did "sell and furnish intoxicating liquor" in violation of Vermont law. O'Neil was arrested and pleaded not guilty.

This jolly traffic by a commercial Samaritan had been going on for three years, for O'Neil was a hospitable Hibernian with a flourishing wine and liquor business over the border. He was the darling of tippling Vermonters in Manchester, East Dorset, and Rutland, and his method was as innocent as it was open.

Customers could order by express or mail; if they were *in extremis*, by telegraph. Express was a favorite of old soaks who simply gave O'Neil's handsome jug to the National Express Company in Rutland to have it returned from Whitehall filled with hooch. This gay-looking bit of crockery displayed the name and business of O'Neil, so that rum-running across the border was hardly secretive. Knowing drinking folks, O'Neil's sole caution was that most of his orders went C.O.D.

But Vermont's liquor laws were stern, denying the right to

65

"sell, furnish or give away intoxicating liquors." This was the delight of Prohibitionists, the clergy and bootleggers. Cider was exempt, on the grounds that it was used for Communion. For the better prevention of scandal the prohibition did not extend to tippling in private homes. But the word "give" in the statute forbade guzzling by persons at public celebrations, Fourth of July, barn-raisings and firemen's musters. The word "furnish" applied to persons bringing liquor into the state for sale. For each offense the first conviction was $10 plus costs; the second was $20 and one month in prison; the third and subsequent convictions, $20 and not less than three or more than six months in jail.

It was on the number of offenses that John O'Neil came a cropper. For the vigilant drys laid almost five hundred cases (if not jugs) before Justice of the Peace Bailey of Rutland. He found O'Neil guilty of four hundred and fifty-seven such offenses and levied a fine of $9,140 and $472.96 costs. In addition O'Neil was to be "confined at hard labor in the Rutland House of Correction for the term of a month, and in case such fine and costs were not paid on or before the expiration of one month he should be confined at hard labor for a term of 28,836 days" [seventy-nine years].

O'Neil appealed to the county court where a jury found him guilty. County Judge Veazey weighed the sentence. A colonel in General Winfield Scott Hancock's Army of the Potomac, Wheelock G. Veazy was credited with having stopped Pickett's charge at Gettysburg. A grateful President Harrison later appointed him to the Interstate Commerce Commission. As a judge he had none of the charity of Solomon, for he held that O'Neil must serve a reduced fifty-four years if his fine were not paid. So the poor fellow appealed to the Supreme Court in Montpelier.

Seven judges heard such worthies as J. C. Baker for O'Neil, Prout and Walker for the National Express Company and W. C. Dutton and L. H. Thompson for the state. O'Neil's chief argument was that the sale took place in New York, hence Vermont had no jurisdiction. But Chief Judge Homer E. Royce writing the opinion for a unanimous court, upheld the sentence. He reasoned that the place of sale was determined by the intention of the parties, and since the liquor was sent C.O.D. there was a condition precedent attached to the sale: Neither party expected it to be completed until the buyer gave his money in Vermont to the Rutland express agent; O'Neil had no intention of relinquishing title to the liquor when he gave it to the express man. It was as if goods were entrusted to a clerk with instructions not to turn the package over until he got the money. One might speculate further and say that if the liquor had been destroyed in transit, surely the Vermont purchasers would not be expected to pay for it.

In desperation O'Neil appealed to the United States Supreme Court with a new argument. The Eighth Amendment to the Constitution forbids "cruel and unusual punishments," as does the Constitution of Vermont. This argument appealed to Mr. Justice Field. For many pages he waxed indignant that Vermont should give "fifty-four years at hard labor for these transactions which no power of human intellect can accurately describe as anything

but interstate commerce." Such punishment, he opined, was comparable to "torture, the rack or thumb-screw"; moreover, this was "six times as great as any Vermont court could have imposed for manslaughter, forgery, perjury and greater than the maximum for burglary or highway robbery."

As a transplanted New Englander, Justice Field found another of O'Neil's arguments that appealed to him: that the transaction was interstate commerce and as such, Federal jurisdiction took precedence over Vermont. "Orders are sent all over the country," he wrote; "to California for fruits and wine, to Kentucky for whiskies . . . and amazement would strike the large class of merchants engaged in transmitting goods from one portion of the country to another, if they were told that they were thereby rendered liable to the penal statutes of the states to which the goods were sent in compliance with the orders of the purchasers." He further reasoned that if the contract had merely been initiated in New York and not consummated until the goods reached Vermont, this was indeed interstate commerce. Justice Field's nephew, Justice Brewer, and Justice Harlan, grandfather of the present Justice Harlan, agreed. But the majority of the court took a dim view of this reasoning.

The majority agreed with the Vermont court that this was not

interstate commerce and brushed off the cruel-and-unusual-punish-
ment argument. This was merciful relief, for in those balmy days
of relatively few cases the nine Washington solons were prone to
prolixity if not high wind.

By contrast Vermont opinions were models of epitome. Chief
Judge Royce had served in Congress for two terms and, though he
had spoken only twice, he was known as the Silver-tongued
Vermonter. His sole reply to cruel and unusual punishment was
that if the penalty had been for a single offense the argument
might have merit, but O'Neil had committed "a great number of
offenses." Such brevity typified the best Vermont tradition, illustrated by the story of the Vermont judge in the barber's chair:
"How would you like your hair cut, Judge?" inquired the barber.
"In silence," replied His Honor.

As to the fate of John O'Neil, we know only that after the
United States Supreme Court had spoken, he became Prisoner
#3567 in Rutland's House of Correction. How long he had to
remain in durance vile is lost in antiquity.

The Vampire's Heart

ROCKWELL STEPHENS

In the Fall of 1890 there appeared on the first page of Woodstock's weekly newspaper, *The Vermont Standard*, a story that might well have come out of the seventeenth instead of the nineteenth century. On Page 1 of the issue of October 9, under the single arresting headline VAMPIRISM IN WOODSTOCK was the following, which we give verbatim:

The following remarkable story is reprinted here as given in the *Boston Transcript*. A further elucidation of the matter is furnished below.

Even in New England curious and interesting material may be found among old people descended from the English colonial settlers. About five years ago an old lady told me that, fifty years before our conversation, the heart of a man was burned on Woodstock Green, Vermont. The man had died of consumption six months before and the body buried in the ground. A brother of the deceased fell ill soon after and in a short time it appeared that he, too, had consumption; when this became known the family decided at once to disinter the body of the dead man and examine his heart. They did so, and found the heart undecayed, and containing liquid blood. Then they reinterred the body, took the heart to the middle of Woodstock Green, where they kindled a fire under an iron pot, in which they placed the heart and burned it to ashes.

The old lady who told me this was living in Woodstock at the time, and said she saw the disinterrment and burning with her own eyes.

The Woodstock writer, who fails to disclose his source of information, continues and embellishes the account as follows:

We may as well help the old lady's recollections in this matter and fill in with further details what she has left incomplete. To be particular in

71

72

dates, the incident happened about the middle of June, 1830. The name of the family concerned was Corwin, and they were near relatives of the celebrated Thomas Corwin, sometime Senator in Congress from Ohio, well known for his wit and attractiveness as an orator. The body disinterred was buried in the Cushing Cemetery. With regard to the cause of the illness that had seized the brother of the deceased, there was a general consensus of opinion among all the physicians at that time practicing in Woodstock. These embraced the honored names of Dr. Joseph A. Gallup, Dr. Burnwell, Dr. John D. Powers, Dr. David Palmer, Dr. Willard who recently died in New York, not to mention other members of the profession at that time residing in Woodstock and held in high repute at home and abroad. These all advised the disinterrment as above described, all being clearly of the opinion that this was a case of assured vampirism. Only there was a slight controversy between Drs. Gallup and Powers as to the exact time that the brother of the deceased was taken with consumption. Dr. Gallup asserted that the vampire began his work before the brother died. Dr. Powers was positively sure that it was directly after.

The boiling of the pot on Woodstock Green, spoken of by the old lady, was attended by a large concourse of people. The ceremonies were conducted by the selectmen, attended by some of the prominent citizens of the village then residing on the common. It will suffice to name the Honorable Norman Williams, General Lyman Mower, General Justus Durdick, B. F. Mower, Walter Palmer, Esq., Woodward R. Fitch, of old men of renown, sound-minded fathers among the community, discreet careful men. The old lady has forgotten to state what was done with the pot and its ghastly collection of dust after the ceremonies were over. A hole ten feet square and fifteen feet deep was dug right in the center of the park where the fire had been built, the pot with the ashes was placed in the bottom, and then on top of that was laid a block of solid granite weighing seven tons, cut out of Knox Ledge. The hole was then filled up with dirt, the blood of a bullock was sprinkled on the fresh earth, and the fathers then felt that vampirism was extinguished forever in Woodstock. Eight or ten years after these events some curious-minded persons made excavations in the Park, if by chance anything might be found of the pot. They dug down fifteen feet, but found nothing. Rock, pot, ashes and all had disappeared. They heard a roaring noise, however, as of some great conflagration, going on in the bowels of the earth, and a smell of sulphur began to fill the cavity, whereupon, in some alarm they hurried to the surface, filled up the hole again, and went their way. It is reported that considerable disturbance took place on the surface of the ground for several days, where the hole had been dug, some rumblings and shaking of the earth, and some smoke was emitted.

What to make of this grisly tale? Witch-craft in the nineteenth century? Preposterous! An exorcism such as this in a community as prosperous as Woodstock in the 1830's? Did none of the "sound-minded fathers among the community, discreet careful men" make protest at a rite of medieval sorcery in a town boasting many doctors, a young medical college, and more than the usual number of men of outstanding talent and industry?

In fairness to the "prominent citizens" and to the doctors we may examine this fantastic story in the light of its time. Superstition, though no longer a guiding principle, had by no means been scotched by either church or science. The eighteenth century is heavily documented with nostrums and practices to ward off evil — natural and supernatural. The last witch had been hanged in Salem long before, but like folk music, the mythology lingered on for another century and more.

As late as 1750 a treatise on vampirism written in Europe in 1734 was translated into English and widely read as an aftermath of a period when all Europe was filled with reports of the exploits of vampires. They were supposed to be the souls of dead men which quit the buried bodies by night to suck the blood of living persons. Hence when the vampire's grave is opened, his body is found to be fresh and rosy from the blood consumed.

Such progress as medicine had made by our year 1830 had done but little to enlighten a rural population. Despite an unavailing voice here and there, the period saw a flowering of nostrums, many liberally laced with one-hundred-proof alcohol, which were an accepted part of every home medicine chest for another generation at least.

Could the medical men of the town in fact have concurred in their verdict of "an assured case of vampirism"? One can speculate that they felt they were dealing, as in undoubtedly many other cases, with *force majeur;* that protest would only deepen the suspicions against which they constantly worked.

Who were these medical men and what was their training? Dr.

Joseph A. Gallup, one of the founders of Woodstock's Vermont Medical College, was considered the leading physician of eastern Vermont. He was one of the few then practicing who, as a member of the Dartmouth College medical school's first graduating class, had had any formal training. The author of several books, including an appendix on consumption, he was "highly praised for his experimental knowledge." He was president of the medical college on its establishment in 1826 and gave all the lectures for several years.

Evidently a man of firm and outspoken opinion, he became the leader of a faction which apparently created a controversy sufficiently widespread to merit comment in a Rhode Island doctor's essay on medical delusions. Dr. Gallup's party of New England medical men contended that the general character of diseases of the time were inflammatory, and hence blood-letting was his "grand remedy." The opposition contended that this general character was essentially opposite, or "asthenic," and they relied largely on opium and brandy in treating diseases.

Castigating the "asthenics," Gallup is quoted: "It is probable that for forty years past, opium and its preparations have done seven times the injury that they have rendered benefit on the great scale of the world." The opposition: "The lancet is a weapon that annually slays more than the sword;" and "the King of Great Britain loses more subjects every year by this means than the battle and campaign of Waterloo cost him with all its glories."

Like many another of his time, Dr. Gallup evidently had an eye for business, and we find him the joint proprietor of a drugstore in the town. A regular feature of the advertising columns of Woodstock's *Weekly Observer* was nearly half a column extolling "Essence of Life — a valuable medicine discovered by Dr. Jona. Moore, a very worthy physician of Putney, Vermont . . . [which] . . . has stood unrivalled amidst the downfall of hundreds of medicines which have been offered to the public as specifics for the same diseases (as indicated on the label) and has been the means of snatching thousands from the jaws of death.

"This Essence answers a valuable purpose in almost every case of debility, and there are few if any diseases which do not arise from that source. It may be given to either sex and at any period if weakness prevail, the composition being entirely derived from the vegetable kingdom."

This modest statement is followed by a heartfelt endorsement by ministers of the gospel in Putney, Dummerston, Westminster, and Brattleboro. The advertisement concludes with the lines: "Dr. Moore's Essence of Life — for sale, wholesale and retail at the store of Gallup and Taylor — Woodstock."

Of the other doctors listed as concurring in the judgment of vampirism, Dr. John D. Powers was perhaps more typical of his time. He had learned his medicine from his father, Stephen Powers, who in turn got his training from older doctors in Massachusetts between 1750 and 1755, and who moved to Woodstock with the first families in 1774. Dr. John is assumed by some local historians to have ousted Dr. Gallup as head of the Vermont Medical College — which was obliged to close in '61 — and was said to be "rather old-fashioned." It is perhaps significant that he disagreed with Dr. Gallup on whether the victim of our vampire fell ill before or after the malignant creature's death.

Dr. John Burnell, whom the author of our story indentifies as "Burnwell," came to Woodstock in 1809, boarded for a time with Dr. Gallup, and planned to take Dr. Gallup's practice, as he was busy with the store, but Burnell evidently was disappointed in this hope. He nevertheless made his reputation in the community by his successes in a "lung fever" epidemic in 1813, and was noted as one of the earliest practitioners of vaccination. An advertisement in the *Observer* of 1820 informs that "Kine Pock vaccine is effective in preventing Small Pox" and that "Dr. Burnell will vaccinate any who call for it." Dana's *History of Woodstock* says, "Dr. Burnell always felt the greatest interest in the advancement of medical science as opposed to quackery and empiricism," and asserts he "had a truly scientific mind."

We can only speculate whether one of the town doctors conducted the dissection of this vampire heart, said to have been found "undecayed and containing liquid blood." The dissection would have been welcomed by one of the medical students, whose supply of cadavers was so limited that grave-robbing had become the cause of contemporary outcry. The practice was evidently so frequent that the medical school had been forced to make a public

promise "not to use any human body which might be disinterred hereabout."

The question of "liquid blood" raises a nice point. It is in the tradition of true vampirism that the creature's heart contain blood drawn from its victims. Our tale avers that this vampire's death occurred some six months before the exorcism. What does pathology say about the stated presence of liquid blood existing in a body six months after death?

"Impossible — strictly speaking," say all three of Woodstock's practicing physicians today. "But," asks the layman, probing, "might there be fluid of a sort, perhaps discolored, which a person predisposed to find blood, would think of as blood?" Two votes for "Yes — maybe."

The list of "prominent citizens of the village then residing on the common" is perfectly valid. It would also be in keeping that the ceremonies be conducted by the selectmen, though these, three in number as of today, were not named. Town records identify them as John A. Pratt, Jason Kendall, and Nathan T. Churchill.

Did any of these leave a journal that might throw light on the occasion? If so, it is still buried in some attic trunk. But this line of inquiry at last produced virtually unimpeachable evidence of the continuing existence of the key superstition on which the story is based.

In the stacks of the Norman Williams Public Library on Woodstock Green — and incidentally on the site of the one-time home of the Honorable Norman Williams listed as an observer — is a folder containing some seventy typed pages, labeled "Memoirs of Daniel Ransom." There are short biographical outlines of various members of the Ransom family, one of the very earliest to settle in the town and distinguished for a succession of outstanding men in every generation.

The following is copied from Page 20:

Frederick Ransom, the second son of my father and mother, was born in South Woodstock, Vermont, June 16, 1797, and died of consumption February 14th, 1817, at the age of about twenty. He had a good education and was a member of Dartmouth College at the time of his death. My rememberance of him is quite limited as I was only three years at the time of his death and I date my rememberance of anything at a visit of Dr. Frost to Frederick in his sickness. Keeping shy of the Doctor, fearing he would freeze me.

It has been related to me that there was a tendency in our family to consumption, and that I, who now in 1894 am over eighty years old, would die with it before I was thirty. It seems that Father shared somewhat in the idea of hereditary diseases and withal had some superstition, for it was said that if the heart of one of the family who died of consumption was taken out and burned, others would be free from it. And Father, having some faith in the remedy, had the heart of Frederick taken out after he had been buried, and it was burned in Captain Pearson's blacksmith forge. However, it did not prove a remedy for mother, sister, and two brothers died with that disease afterward.

Mother did indeed die, of consumption (as tuberculosis was then called) in 1821, followed by sister in 1828 and other brothers in 1830 and 1832.

Here, in any event, is a case of exorcism only thirteen years prior to our story. How many others took place in those years when consumption, diagnosed as such or simply labeled "fever," was a major killer—when doctors were generally mistrusted, and medical science was just beginning to emerge from the dark ages?

There is little doubt that the connection between a burned heart and consumption was a widespread belief springing from medieval times and persisting well into the nineteenth century. In his *Doctors of the American Frontier* Richard Dunlop says, "The fried heart of a rattlesnake could be eaten to cure consumption along most of the frontier as it moved westward."

The ritualistic concept of blood is practically a contemporary survival. The sprinkling of blood or ashes of a sacrificial animal has been an accepted rite of purification from medieval times. Hence in embellishing our tale the author naturally felt it appropriate that when the hole in which our vampire's heart burned was filled, "the blood of a bullock was sprinkled on the fresh earth."

So how stands our cast for belief or disbelief in this grisly tale? The case fits the times, the cast of characters is established, but what of our accused — one Corwin, male, torn from his grave in the Nathan Cushing Cemetery in the Town of Woodstock on that June day of 1830?

The cemetery is there, above the north bank of the Ottauquechee stream, flanked on the south and west by town roads and the east and north by the pastures and mowings of a modern dairy farm. But among the headstones dating to the early days of the town, none bears the name Corwin. Nor does the careful script on the pages of the Town register of births and deaths record a Corwin.

The name is not found in census or land records of Woodstock or the adjacent Pomfret — which also used Cushing plots.

So speculation ends, as it often must, with a question mark. And we may take this tale or leave it, or file it as a testimonial of the tragic helplessness of families of those times when faced with the mysteries of sickness and death.

Money, Injustice & Bristol Bill

STEPHEN GREENE

More than a century ago, Groton, in Caledonia County, boasted twice as many sheep as cattle, but the cattle still outnumbered the people, of whom there were some nine hundred. There were seven sawmills in town then, and a cloth-fulling mill, and of course a gristmill. There were two tanneries, two churches and two stores. Although the terrain was rough and the soil stony, Groton produced oats on the order of 13,000 bushels yearly and the maples yielded ten tons of sugar. In short Groton in 1850 was a typical Vermont farming community. Probably, like other small towns, a poor place to come if you didn't want to be noticed. Certainly not the place if you wanted to mind your own business — and your business was, in the simplest possible way, just to make money.

It was dead of Winter when the five newcomers arrived. First a fiercely bearded figure of about forty, short and broad shouldered, with noticeably piercing blue eyes. He was accompanied by a short stout man battered about the face. They both had British accents. A few days later another Englishman came to town, tall and long-nosed, a nervous man obviously, but with a more winning expression than either of his compatriots. It was a matter of sympathetic interest when the tall Englishman one chilly day welcomed his attractive wife and baby. And not long after this the bearded one was joined by a woman in her twenties, apparently determined to become a farmwife despite her looks and her dash and her musical ways.

The lanky Britisher and his wife and child stayed with Peter Paul, Groton carpenter and man-of-all-work. The first two arrivals, with the younger woman, moved to a farm out in West Groton

81

belonging to one Ephraim Low. They all lived quietly, visited the village seldom, and made no effort to associate one with another in public. In fact, when two of the men came in for a drink at McLean Marshall's blacksmith shop, one would make a point of jumping off the sleigh outside the village and strolling in later. To rural Groton such maneuvers seemed fairly extreme, but maybe the newcomers had reasons for being unobtrusive. They had.

No matter how imaginative the speculation as to the occupations and identities of these visitors — and we can assume today that it ranged widely: what could you expect of foreigners who arrive in town in mid-Winter? — it paled beside the truth. For the new arrivals, in order of appearance, were William (Bristol Bill) Warburton, alias William Darlington, British-born burglar already known to the police of both Boston and New York; George (English Jim) Green, burglar and part-time professional prize fighter; Christian Meadows, engraver and thief; Mrs. Meadows, a housewife and mother as modest as she seemed, and a former

cabaret singer named Margaret O'Connor who, although she was to pass in Vermont as Mrs. Warburton, was known in New York underworld circles as Gookin Peg.

Thus the good town of Groton became unwittingly the residence of what a newspaper was to call some of the most noted and accomplished rogues in America. But they didn't come to town to be burglars or pugilists or cabaret singers — but to try, as inconspicuously and effectively as possible, to make money.

The whole thing had started the previous Spring. Ephraim Low, who had failed in business as a storekeeper, persuaded Meadows, then working for a Boston printer, to steal a set of bank-note dies with a view to setting up in counterfeiting. Making and passing bogus notes was a popular and even rewarding pursuit, for many banks were empowered to issue their own negotiable bills, and these were so numerous and so varied in design that the average man couldn't possibly distinguish the homemade article from the real thing. Counterfeits were of two kinds: they were either made from scratch, or were genuine bills from which the figures would be removed and replaced by other figures with more digits. The latter variant of do-it-yourself money was, in the master plan of Ephraim Low, to be the specialty of the venture — informal, ill-designed and wholly unsuccessful — which became known locally as the "Groton Bank." Christian Meadows, according to Low's table of organization, was to be engraver and chief printer. Bristol Bill and English Jim Green were engaged to pass the upgraded notes.

But although Meadows was given the leading role in the Groton Bank, Warburton soon emerged as the principal actor. This charming villain — the black sheep, if we are to believe his biographer, of a well-known British family, and an alumnus of the Australian penal colony at Botany Bay — has perhaps best been characterized by Stephen Royce, one of three Vermont governors who were to be involved with his future, as a man "combining with strong and excitable passions a quick and deep sense of what he assumes to be justice and injustice." And from the moment that he set foot on Green Mountain soil Bristol Bill felt that justice was not his, and that the world, in the persons of northern Vermonters, conspired against him.

Obviously his initial mistake was to leave the city, and the reader who will put up with a brief excursion into some earlier criminal history will probably agree. Bristol Bill would never have left New York if Sam Drury, an Astoria, Long Island, receiver of stolen goods, had not taken umbrage at the role Bill played in what the *Police Gazette* called the Pandora's Box Case. It seems that Drury had attempted to eliminate a lawyer of his acquaintance by sending him a package designed to explode when unwrapped. Warburton, together with a man named William (One-Eyed) Thompson, had co-operated with the police to dupe Drury into an admission of guilt — at a "rat council," as the *Gazette* dubbed the thieves' conference overheard by police. In retaliation Drury had quickly succeeded in pulling strings to have Thompson jailed; Warburton fled from his wrath — and ended up in remote Groton, Vermont.

Bill was not an insensitive man, and surely must have felt from the beginning that things were not going as they should in Vermont. It became apparent that Low, a failure as a storekeeper, was not cut out to be a counterfeiter either: the printing equipment he had assembled in Groton proved on inspection to be neither adequate nor complete. So while Meadows and Peter Paul, one of the local hirelings, attempted to tinker the old machinery into shape, and while Low hustled off to Boston for spare parts, Bill fumed and observed darkly that he had not ventured into this nowhere just to putter. He still intended, he told someone, to do a job "in great style." Therefore he must have thought his luck had turned when he heard that the State bank commissioners were expected in St. Johnsbury, to collect deposits on shares of the soon-to-open Passumpsic Bank. Here was the job to fill his time and his pocketbook. With a kit of burglar's tools under arm, and with Peg and English Jim in tow, off he went to cash in at last.

He was encouraged further when he arrived at St. Johnsbury's friendly Hull Curtis Hotel. No need to be self-effacing here. The place was teeming with officials and townspeople, relaxing in an atmosphere of ready-made money, and plenty of it. With practiced technique he established Peg in the hotel parlor and, while she entranced the company with song, accompanying herself on the piano, he and Jim went upstairs to rifle the suitcase of the commissioner most likely to have the deposits in his safekeeping. It contained old clothes. With a returning sense of frustration, they searched for the room that held the money — and discovered that it was being watched round the clock by two armed guards. Bill packed up his tools, fetched Peg from the piano, and the trio went back to Groton.

This was the first of the letdowns that Warburton was to suffer during his six years in Vermont. During the next six weeks and in a growing state of disillusionment, he took one or another of his colleagues on visits to banks in Irasburg, Standstead — over the border in Quebec — Chelsea, Montpelier and Danville. All proved to have night watchmen, or at least employees who slept in. At Wells River they did manage to loosen the bank's outside shutters before they were obliged to depart empty-handed.

It was more than discouraging, it was unfair. Despite energy, willing help and skills learned as a big-time operator, he was stymied at every turn by a fate as cranky as the Green Mountain countryside.

Indeed, by early March the burglary business in Vermont had proved so unprofitable, and the counterfeiting under Low's inept direction so unlikely to accelerate to even a snail's pace, that the partners in crime had had it: English Jim returned to the city, taking with him, Bill was to complain afterwards, his (Bill's) own set of handcrafted skeleton keys. Warburton, by now a very unhappy man was planning to do exactly the same thing.

But Bill was late. At 10 o'clock the night of March 12 a posse of

White River officers knocked at the door of the house where he and Peg were staying and placed the two under arrest. Bill went quietly, but told all concerned that had Green been present the outcome would have been different — a statement which, in the light of events, was probably entirely true. Meadows, Mrs. Meadows and the three local confederates — McLean Marshall, Paul and Low — were picked up the same night, together with variously hidden loot that included one-hundred-and-fifteen steel dies valued at more than $1,000, a transfer press (for making copper plates from the dies), a printing press, and a single bank note from which the denominations had been chemically removed. Among the burglar's tools was a newly and ingeniously conceived machine to cut a hole in the iron safe door of any bank around. This cutter was to arouse considerable interest at the trial.

The trials of Bristol Bill — for there were actually three of them, not including preliminary hearings — proved not only to be the most dramatic in Caledonia County annals, but were also among the longest. The first hearing was held in Groton. Then the prisoners were moved to Danville, the county seat, where the grand jury indicted Low, Marshall, Meadows and Warburton — the two women were dismissed and Peter Paul had turned state's evidence — on counts embracing possession of "certain burglarious tools," and counterfeiting. Bail was set too high to be raised and the defendants were returned to the Danville lockup until the June term of court. Low died of pleurisy shortly after the Grand Jury hearing, and the prisoners, now reduced to three, occupied the three-month wait each in his own fashion. Marshall brooded over his predicament; the obliging Meadows made artistic engravings for jail visitors, and Bill wrote letters. Several, which unfortunately have not survived, were addressed to Justice Burbank, who had presided at the first hearing. He wrote one to District Attorney John McKeon, in New York City, claiming that One-Eyed Thompson and not Drury was responsible for the Pandora's Box explosion, and that the "rat council" that implicated Drury "was a foul and black conspiracy, got up by the said Wm. H. Thompson for the purpose of convicting Drury, and thereby save himself." If he, McKeon, would get Warburton out of Vermont, Bill promised to come back to New York and tell them all about it. When this produced no results, Warburton wrote a letter of much the same import to Drury's lawyer.

But Warburton's pastimes during his enforced lay-over in Danville were not wholly literary. Ever the professional, he fashioned a cell-door key from an old stovepipe; then, when he was ready to make the break, let fellow-prisoner McLean Marshall in on his scheme. But Marshall feigned a crippling attack of indigestion on the night of the escape, and the next day had a chat with the State's Attorney. In addition to telling about Bill's key, he arranged to join Paul in testifying for the prosecution.

Thus when the first trial finally got under way, at 8:30 on the morning of June 12, just two prisoners came in: with Low dead and Paul and Marshall turning state's evidence, only Bill and Christian Meadows were left to face the charges. The courtroom, in the best tradition of tribunal drama, was packed and stifling. Mrs. Meadows, modest and unassuming, and with her babe in arms, sat near her husband, who is reported as "looking scared of his own shadow." Thirty-five-year-old Superior Court Judge Luke Poland presided. William Farrar of Boston, with two other lawyers, represented the defendants; bespectacled Bliss Davis, a local man with a reputation as a no-holds-barred advocate, headed the prosecution staff.

Counsel for Meadows moved straightway that the case be continued to the next session of court, since needed witnesses were not then available. Counsel for Warburton also moved to continue the case on the grounds that the number of counts in the indictment against him was not justified by the evidence produced at the March hearing. Both motions were denied.

The respondents then being arraigned in due form, the clerk read the indictment: possessing plates and dies for the purpose of counterfeiting bank bills on certain banks. A wan Christian Meadows pleaded not guilty. Bill Warburton, the picture of health and confidence, pleaded not guilty in that name, "and as to the other name" — he had also been indicted under the alias of William Darlington — "I know nothing about it."

The jury was empaneled, Davis made his opening statement, and called Peter Paul as his first witness against Meadows. Paul told how Low had approached him early in 1849 about his counterfeiting scheme, how Low had lined up the necessary equipment and had found a mysterious "Mr. M." to work it. With such a setup, Low vowed, they would all make their fortunes.

After a witness had told how engraving tools had been found in March in the house Meadows occupied, William Wilson was called to the stand. Wilson was the Boston printer and engraver from whom Meadows had stolen the dies in 1849. He described how he secured the backing of the New England Association for the Detection of Counterfeiters, then spent a year in fruitless search until a sister-in-law of Meadows told him she thought the engraver lived at the end of some railway line up north. Inquiries in White River led him to Groton, he said.

During the cross examination of Wilson occurred the trial's only note of recorded humor. Wilson and Farrar were accusing one another of a friendship with the unsavory One-Eyed Thompson when the judge remarked, "very happily" as one reporter puts it, "The gentlemen had better not expose themselves too much here."

Other witnesses told of the mutilated bank note, obviously in the process of alteration, found between the leaves of Low's diary.

There was a stir in the courtroom when McLean Marshall took the stand, for it was known that he, far more than Paul, had been in the inner circle of the confederates. Warburton, who had been busily taking notes on the testimony up to this point, for the first time looked a little less than his confident self. A motion to exclude Marshall from giving evidence being denied, the erstwhile tavernkeeper-blacksmith proceeded to unfold the whole story: The ring had been organized by Low; Warburton and English Jim Green had been hired to pass the notes and, together with Meadows and Low, were to share in the profits. When the counterfeiting scheme bogged down and the jimmies and safe-cracking tools arrived in Groton, it was arranged that, as a stopgap, they all become partners in Warburton's business (i.e., burglary) too. One thousand dollars in genuine bills of small denomination — the counterfeiters' raw material — had been collected, Marshall said, but Low's sister-in-law had intercepted them.

The defense lawyers were on their feet continually to object to such damaging testimony, but the government men were equally determined, and bit by bit all loopholes were plugged. Finally several witnesses testified that they had seen Warburton, Meadows, Low and the others together at various times. The government rested.

The only witnesses for the defense were three of the White River posse who testified that Warburton and Peg O'Connor had indeed been ready to leave town at the time of the arrest. Neither Bill nor Meadows took the stand.

The arguments of counsel — there were four of them — were long and spirited, according to reports, but were not reported in detail by the local press. "Suffice it to say," one reporter has written annoyingly, "that they were very able and ingenious on both sides." We know now that the argument by Davis, "a very sarcastic man" one contemporary described him, must have been particularly telling. During the lawyers' speeches, tears would sometimes come to the eyes of Mrs. Meadows, whose expression, the *Caledonian* thought, "pleads harder and stronger for her husband's acquittal than evidence or counsel can do." Judge Poland then committed the case to the jury in a charge that was "fair, impartial and able." The jury was out all night and part of the following morning, finally bringing in a verdict of guilty against both defendants.

Warburton was immediately arraigned again on four burglary counts in connection with his attempted holdups. A parade of witnesses identified him with the tools, especially with the giant cutter which Oscar C. Hale, cashier of the Bank of Newbury, now demonstrated. He showed how the point could be driven into the keyhole or hinges of an iron vault door; then, using this as a pivot, how a hole four inches in diameter could be cut. "I don't think there is a bank door in the state that could stand up against it," he declared with relish.

But Marshall was again the chief witness and his testimony was again damaging. He told how the would-be burglars had successively visited many of the banks in that area, and for what purpose. The second trial lasted a day and a half, and Warburton was found guilty on three of the four counts.

At the Danville trials the foreigners were taken to lunch at the nearby hotel, where their appearances were a treat for many who had not been able to get into the courtroom. Even today one Danville resident remembers her mother telling her that Bristol Bill appeared a "rough-looking man" and Meadows "very much of a gentleman." Writing of Bill after many years, one onlooker could "seem to hear now, after the lapse of half a century, the rattling of the chains as he shuffled across Danville Green."

But three days later, when the men came back for sentencing, the lucky ones who got in witnessed the most exciting scene of all. The prisoners entered the courtroom, after being given the usual routine search; and the judge asked if they had anything to say. Bristol Bill certainly had. And if Sheriff Evans would remove his handcuffs, he would consult his notes.

Then he reviewed the history of the trials. Marshall, he said, was an acknowledged perjurer and should never have been allowed to testify. Shaking his finger at Davis, Bill added, "Your pupil, Mr. State's Attorney, made an appearance on the witness stand creditable to the instructions of his master." Moreover, Warburton went on, the grounds for including him in the counterfeiting indictment were wholly insufficient. In any case the entire output of the Groton Bank was a single bill from which the figures had been removed; no actual counterfeiting had taken place. The trials, he said, were an outrage on judicial procedure. It was generally agreed that Bill's presentation was a masterly one.

Judge Poland heard him out, then sentenced each of the two men to ten years at hard labor in the State Prison at Windsor.

Meadows appeared to be stricken by the sentence, and his wife comforted him. State's Attorney Davis crossed to Meadows and leaned down to speak to him.

Suddenly a knife appeared in the hands of Warburton. Yelling "Take that!" he plunged it, from the right and rear, into the neck of the prosecutor. Davis, staggered by the blow, fell to the floor. He thought at first that the stem of his glasses had become embedded in his neck, but when he realized what had happened he was heard to murmur "I am killed."

The courtroom sat paralyzed for a moment as the lawyer, struggling on the floor, attempted to pull the knife out. Then Constable Coffrin did it for him. Someone ran up to the Judge, crying, "Davis is murdered!" Meadows moved as far from the

91

scene of violence as his leg irons would permit. Bristol Bill stood unmoved while the court officers secured him, and Farrar slipped the handcuffs back on his wrists.

"It looks like you've killed Davis," the lawyer said. Bill's reply was in character:

"If I could do the same for Marshall, I'd die happy."

His feelings on this occasion echoed those of another British ruffian with a grievance more than one-hundred years before. Joseph Blake — or Blueskin, as he was called — was a protege of Jonathan Wild, an icy-hearted and efficient criminal operator who curried favor with the law by turning in those members of his organization whose performance did not come up to his standard. So when Blueskin quarreled with this formidable figure, Wild promptly had him committed to Newgate. On the way to his cell, Blueskin beckoned to Wild as though to speak with him, then cut his throat — "from ear to ear" the account specifies — with a penknife. Although the nature of Davis's wound was different (the knife penetrated to the base of the skull but missed the large veins), the results were similar and equally surprising: both men lived, Wild to end his days fittingly on a Tyburn gallows, the Vermont lawyer to survive to the age of eighty-three.

There was speculation as to where Bill had secured the weapon, a case knife, and how he had succeeded in getting it into the courtroom. It appeared that he had smuggled it from the hotel dining table, had broken off the handle and hidden the blade in a handkerchief which he held in his hand when searched.

Thus, on a note of violence, an end was written to the brief history of the Groton Bank. But the actors in the drama had the rest of their lives to lead, and if none enjoyed such a long old age as did Bliss Davis — at one point surely the worst of actuarial risks — at least their later years were not uneventful.

For William Wilson, the persistent printer, everything turned out pretty well. After safely returning his dies to Boston, he billed the New England Association for the Detection of Counterfeiters for $1,113.77 to cover his services and expenses — and collected.

Ten years after the Danville trials, Luke Poland was named Chief Justice of the Vermont Supreme Court. From this important seat he was appointed to fill an unexpired two-year term in the

United States Senate, and for eight more years he served in the House of Representatives. During his decade in Washington, Poland was chairman of commissions that exposed the Credit Mobilier and the Ku Klux Klan. Perhaps his greatest achievement was to head the first legislative committee to undertake the task of compiling the Federal laws.

Christian Meadows had not long occupied his cell in Windsor before efforts were under way to get him a pardon. At the request of the New Hampshire Agricultural Society he engraved a diploma which included the old elm on the Daniel Webster homestead. When the aging New Hampshire statesman saw it, and was informed that its artist-craftsman was in Vermont's state penitentiary, he was moved to ask, "Why do you bury your best talents in your state prisons?" and he assured one of those working for Meadows's release that employment could be found for the engraver in Washington at the Smithsonian Institution, or at the State, War or Navy departments.

But Webster had died when Governor Erastus Fairbanks, on July 4, 1853, not only granted a pardon but contributed $100 toward the purchase price of a house in Windsor for the engraver. There according to a correspondent writing in 1880, Meadows lived "a life of substantial reform" and "died some years ago." Several of Meadows's engravings are still in existence, notably a handsome one of the Dartmouth College campus.

Bristol Bill, hustled off to Windsor in "a very complete set of irons," had of course a third trial to face as a result of his attack on Davis. This he succeeded in postponing, to allow the legislature to pass on the question of change of venue in such cases. Therefore when Stephen Royce became Governor in 1854, Warburton was still at Windsor and still untried for the attack on Davis.

In May of 1855, Governor Royce wrote Bliss Davis his estimate of Warburton's character quoted earlier — that Bill was a passionate man of strong convictions — and went on to say that "when such a spirit is to be dealt with in the way of punishment, it is especially important that he should know his punishment to be just, instead of believing that he is made to suffer under oppression." The Governor pointed out that Warburton had already served a longer portion of his sentence than was usual, and told Davis he was inclined to do one of two things: either release him outright, under condition that he leave the state for good, or have him up for trial for assault on Davis.

The former State's Attorney subsequently visited Bill at Windsor, and must have told him that a factor in the case was Mrs. Davis's fear for her husband's life if Warburton were to be released. The next day Bill, a man as we know given to correspondence, wrote to Mrs. Davis. The letter is now preserved in the Fairbanks Museum in St. Johnsbury and could well serve as a model of how to say you're sorry (five years later) to the wife of a man you've knifed in the neck.

"Much respected lady," he wrote, "at the friendly interview which took place between me and Mr. Davis yesterday, I was much grieved to hear that I had been the cause of so much grief and anguish to you and your dear children. And feeling at the present much pained at the thought, I felt constrained to address you on the present occasion, to ease your mind and free it from all suspicion of you and yours ever receiving further injury from me.

"Madam, you may perhaps think, as I fear many others do in this neighborhood who do not know me, only by report, that a being who could be guilty of such an act as I have now to answer for, must be totally lost to every finer feeling that belongs to man. But, madam, such an opinion is erroneous. Wherever I am known (Danville excepted) I have ever been looked upon as a man of good disposition, kind and obliging to all — so much so that even my enemies (or rather persons whose opinions were opposed to mine) loved me. And worthy lady, with regard to women and children, my kindly disposition has often carried me beyond my means, and would do so again if I were at liberty." Warburton added that he hoped Mrs. Davis would accept "the enclosed bauble, not for its worth, but as a token of my friendly feelings towards you."

Mrs. Davis wrote back that she was "somewhat surprised that a man who came so very near depriving me of a beloved husband and my children of their father should claim so tender a regard for women and children." She acknowledged the "token of peace" and sent him in return a Bible. "You will oblige me by giving it a daily perusal and by never parting with it." She subscribed her letter "respectfully yours," then, apparently feeling that this was a less than appropriate sentiment, scratched it out and substituted "yours sincerely."

We will never know, unfortunately, what was Bristol Bill's idea of an acceptable bauble. Nor will we know whether Mrs. Davis was finally persuaded of Bill's kindly nature. On June 6, 1856, Warburton underwent his third trial and was pronounced guilty once again. When the judge asked if he had anything to say, Bill did something he had rarely done before: he remained silent. He was sentenced to seven years at hard labor and fined $1 and costs of $51.63.

Four days later he had his pardon and was gone. Apparently the Governor had been given satisfactory assurance that Vermont would see no more of Bill; Bill had long been on record as wanting to see no more of Vermont. At any rate, he dropped from sight. New York police records did not again mention him, and he was replaced in the pages of the *Police Gazette* by younger, more successful operators.

But Groton's bank, which never amounted to much, and Bristol Bill Warburton, whose visit to the state was a downright failure, have not yet been forgotten in Danville.

Eighteen-Hundred-and-Froze-to-Death

SYLVESTER L. VIGILANTE

THE OTHER DAY WE GOT TO TALKING ABOUT COLD. What is the worst weather you can remember? Cold enough to make you move somewhere else? Thirty-five below zero for two weeks straight? Sure, but that was in the Winter time. Let me tell you an awesome tale of a century and a half ago. It sounds like modern fiction, but isn't.

Vermont has been referred to jokingly as the place with "ten months of clear sparkling winter, and two months of damn poor sleddin'." This year, the strange year of 1816, the sledding, so to speak, was good all year round: it was the year that neglected to bother with summer.

The Winter had been severe, but the spring began well, the April rains carrying off the last snows from the valleys, and at the end of the month it turned dry and warm. The earth began to come alive, trees blooming, flowers bursting, and the smells of rich dirt and spread manure flooding the countryside.

Harbingers of disaster, however, began to appear in May. It was annoyingly cold, and for Vermont very dry. Some folks blamed the strange times on huge sunspots which were visible to the naked eye for the first time in memory. They were seen first on May third, and again for a few days around June eleventh.

On the fifth of June the weather was hot — about ninety degrees. Then, the next day, the temperature dropped to about forty, and it snowed, although the flakes melted in most places as they struck the ground. It began to get colder, however, and just over in New Hamphsire masons working on a house were forced to halt work when the mortar froze.

Sometime during the evening of June seventh it commenced to

snow again. The snow fell through the night, and, at Waterbury past noon of the eighth. Around Montpelier the snow was more, than a foot deep, and in Cabot, eighteen inches. David Hinman was born on June seventh that year in Derby and, according to family history, on that same day his father had to break ice in the watering trough.

Leaves on the trees were killed, and the beeches remained bare for the rest of the year. Crops that were killed had to be replanted by weary farmers, and most folks were "straight out" in a vain attempt to combat this extraordinary phenomenon. The land was brown, shriveled and bare at a time when the sounds, smells and sights of Summer should have reigned. Songbirds that had not taken shelter, perished. New-shorn sheep froze to death. Vegetation was dead.

And so the "summer" progressed. The ninth of June found ice one-half inch thick on shallow standing water, and icicles a foot long were reported.

In Ryegate most of the corn was destroyed, although some was saved by building fires in the fields. Had it not been for a good crop of oats, many would have been sorely pressed for food. Most people had never tasted oatmeal before; now they were thankful for it.

One of the few people to have any luck that Summer was Abraham Sargent, Jr., who somewhere had obtained seed that produced a very early kind of corn. He moved from Randolph back to his father's farm in Chester, New Hampshire, and there grew "a crop of tolerably sound corn which he sold next spring for four dollars a bushel for seed, and the farmers esteemed it a great favor to obtain it at that price." (The normal price of corn was about one dollar a bushel.) There were also some fair crops of winter wheat, and the price, normally about a dollar a bushel, went up to about three dollars. Seed corn sold for five dollars a bushel in Barnard.

New Englanders were not the only ones with problems. On May thirtieth, there was frost as far south as Virginia, and on July fifth ice was reported in Pennsylvania. The diary of Isaiah Thomas tells us that the "season has been remarkably dry, in the United States generally, and in many parts of Europe — as has the cold also — crops of hay very short."

July fared not much better than June. Just across the Connecticut River, ice was found in a well on July fourth so thick that no water could be obtained save for about a quart from a small hole that had been dug in the ice. It had been there since the end of June, and on July nineteenth a block of ice as large as a washtub was still in evidence. Some parts of New England got rain but Vermont was still dry as a bone.

August stayed cold, and on the twenty-first produced a frost that killed more corn, beans and potatoes. It was felt as far east as Boston. The mountains of Vermont were covered with snow by this time, and many farmers found it impossible to save any crops. By the end of the month frosts were killing Indian corn south into Massachusetts.

In September the mountains were still snow-covered, and the frigid Vermont drought hung on with a grim tenacity. Many areas of the state had been without rain of any worth for one-hundred and twenty days. Fires swept the parched woodlands, smoke blotting out the sun and filling the air with acrid dust. Corn that had somehow survived now received a final blow from a severe frost on September tenth. A few crops of poor quality were harvested, including unripe potatoes from a second planting. They were of little value but better than nothing.

There was much suffering but little if any starvation, as the more fortunate shared with needy neighbors. It was a time of fasting and prayer in the churches — a somber time. Without Summer crops, many did not know where food would come from to last them until Spring.

Bringing in food from the outside areas was difficult. Most of the roads, over mountains and through forests, were very bad. Money, also, was hard to come by. Almost the only source for many was the slow and laborious process of converting trees into salts and potash. This would bring no more than thirty cents for a day's work.

During the Winter, cattle died of starvation for lack of hay. Those poor people who had no "more fortunate neighbors" could not afford the prices that the scanty food was commanding. Fish

100

became the staple diet. Large seines were operated night and day on many of the rivers, and people in eastern Vermont bartered maple sugar for fish. Other items of diet were boiled nettles, wild turnips, boiled leeks, clover heads and porcupines. In New Hampshire 1816 was often referred to as the "Mackerel Year" (other names were "Poverty Year," "Cold Year," and "Famine Year").

The terrible year shook the will and endurance of many, and an exodus to new lands began, many towns being almost deserted. According to Dr. Lewis D. Stilwell in *Migration From Vermont*, folks thought "something . . . had gone permanently wrong with the weather and when this cold season piled itself on top of all preceding afflictions (bad weather had plagued since 1811), a good many Vermonters were ready to quit. Who could blame them?"

The town of Richford was nearly desolate, and, according to one observer, those who remained "nearly starved for want of bread; not an ear of corn fit to roast was raised in town." So few people were left in Worcester that no Town Meetings were held for several years. In 1818 only one family remained. Some were unable to sell their land but they left just the same. Many farms lay fallow for years, until new immigration brought in people who had no memories of the cold years.

Today, real Summers are found in Vermont, and they are as nearly ideal as can be found anywhere in the United States; and Vermont in the summer is just as inviting as it is in the Winter. But now it's a totally separate season.

The Boorn Mystery

RICHARD SANDERS ALLEN

THE LITTLE ROOM above the Manchester jail was stifling in the August heat. The gangling young man sat sweating at the writing table, his face screwed up in an agony of indecision. Around him, unspeaking, stood a Justice of the Peace, a sheriff's deputy and the State's Attorney. These were the three he had asked for. Outside the leaves dropped limply and the long, piercing buzz of a locust came from far off. The man at the table squared his jaw and reached for the quill pen.

The prisoner was named Stephen Boorn, and on this 27th day of August, 1819, he was about to write a detailed confession in one of the strangest cases to be found in criminal history.

Although nobody was aware of it at the time, the noose which was threatening to tighten about Stephen Boorn's neck had begun to dangle seven years before.

At the start of the young republic's second war with Britain, Manchester was a town of some fourteen-hundred people, a trading center for the settlers who had come from Massachusetts and Connecticut to eke out a living on the hillside farms. Among these was the family of Barney Boorn, a respectable man who earned a precarious living by farming, with a little slaughtering and meat-dressing on the side for "hard money." Barney Boorn's brood of five children all grew up in Manchester when it was a poor town. The three boys and two girls were a wild, headstrong bunch whose main pastimes appeared to be quarreling, cussing, and carousing.

The youngest girl, Sally, was married to an older but not steadier neighbor, Russell Colvin. Too shiftless to earn their own keep, the Colvins and their two sons moved in with Sally's father and called it home. When the spirit moved him, which wasn't often, Russell did chores around his father-in-law's farm, and was always Johnny-on-the-spot when the Boorn potatoes were passed.

This state of affairs didn't sit too well with Stephen Boorn, the willful youngest son. He had a wife to support but owned no property. Stephen moved about from one farm to another in Manchester and Dorset, picking up work where he could. Every time he dropped by his parents' home he could see the snug berth that Russell Colvin had made for himself.

To say that Stephen was jealous would be putting it mildly. To friends he muttered that sister Sal was "one of the devil's unaccountables," and Russell was something a great deal worse. Most of the neighbors thought Russell a bit weak-minded, but grudgingly gave him credit for shrewdness in business dealings.

The Colvins had an unusual design for living. Sponging for the most part on patient old Barney Boorn, they would, first one and then the other, take off on unexplained visits elsewhere, visits that lasted from three days to several months. Lewis Colvin, the couple's ten-year-old son, when asked where his father or mother might be, was apt to shrug and say: "Over the mountain."

Then came the day when rotund, blue-eyed Russell Colvin really went over the hill. Not much attention was paid, for Russell's wanderlust was well known. In addition, war with England would be declared in a few weeks, and several young men from town had joined the army. Sally's generous father continued to provide for her, and it was three full years before Sally Colvin commenced to think that it had been a long time since anyone had seen her husband. The war on Lake Champlain was over now. Where in creation had Russell gone to?

When Sally started asking around, tongues began to clack and little sparks of memory began to spin out. Apparently the last time Russell Colvin had been seen was the 10th of May back in 1812. On that Spring morning he had been clearing a field known as the Glazier lot, down near the Battenkill. With him were his son, Lewis, and his brothers-in-law, Stephen and Jesse Boorn. A neighbor was certain he had seen the four lugging rocks to the piles along the edge of the lot. There had been some kind of argument going on among them. Naturally the finger of suspicion swung toward the Boorn boys.

Questioned by self-appointed investigators, Stephen Boorn told various stories about Colvin's disappearance. To one inquiry he said that the man had acted queer and had run off into the woods. To another he replied that Russell was so disgusted, after eating a half-cooked woodchuck prepared by Sally, that he had declared he'd never eat another of her meals. To still other inquisitors both Stephen and Jess denied they were even near the Glazier lot on that particular long-ago day.

But then an old and moldy hat which had belonged to Colvin was found in the lot. Russell was not remembered as a man to bare his thinning locks to the elements. Stephen Boorn chafed and fumed. He declared that Russell Colvin had gone to a hot place, "where potatoes wouldn't freeze."

After the terrible "cold Summer" of 1816 Stephen, with many other Vermont farmers, left town to find a better life in New York State. He settled down some one-hundred-and-sixty miles away in the Adirondack foothill town of Denmark. There he considered himself well shut of the whispers and accusing glances that had followed him about Manchester.

"What could have happened to Russell?" remained a question no one could truly answer. In spite of the general belief that there had been foul play in the Glazier lot, nothing was done. Two more years passed.

It was a supernatural event which started the final delving into the mystery. Stephen's own uncle, Amos Boorn, of all people, reported a horrible dream. As he told it, Russell Colvin appeared at his bedside, declared he had been murdered, and showed him the place where his earthly remains might be found — an old cellar hole in the very lot where he had last been seen. Amos had this unnerving nightmare three times straight.

The character of this particular Boorn was considered unimpeachable, and his neighbors took full stock in his story.

In short order a shovel brigade went pounding down to the little cellar hole in the Glazier lot. Even more sinister now became Stephen's remembered remark about Russell being where potatoes won't freeze. The old cellar had been used for storing them.

The volunteer posse dug and scraped the hole clean, and then sifted the dirt. They found Russell Colvin's jackknife and a button from the coat he had always worn. The web of circumstance tightened still further when a dog and boy, digging in a hollow stump some rods distant, came upon charred bones and what appeared to be two human toenails. At last, after seven years of vague rumors and hearsay, was something tangible for the authorities to act upon.

A court of inquiry convened, presided over by Justice of the Peace Joel Pratt. Four physicians first agreed that the bones were human; argued, and then decided, after viewing the disinterred leg of an amputee, that they were not. But the toenails remained, and at least one of them surely was human, in the doctors' opinion. The inquiry went on for five days, with Russell Colvin's rusty jackknife, his coat button, and a description of his moldering hat the prime evidence. Stephen Boorn's talk about his brother-in-law was taken into account, and it became evident that something, ranging from a mild argument to a battle royal, had taken place in the Glazier lot on May 10, 1812.

Jesse Boorn was questioned thoroughly and was about to be discharged when the Justice showed him Russell Colvin's jackknife one last time. Jesse began to shake and tremble. Then he blurted out that he "believed" his brother, Stephen, had murdered Colvin. If he thought this accusation was going to let him out, he was dead

wrong. Sheriff Heman Robinson clapped him in the Manchester jail and immediately secured a warrant for Stephen's arrest.

Three deputies went over to New York State and brought Stephen back in irons. When confronted with Jesse, Stephen denied everything, but it did little good. With Stephen as principal and Jesse as an accessory, both brothers were held for action of the Grand Jury in September.

As the long, hot Summer wore on, the guilt of the Boorns appeared more and more certain. There were few in town who would say a good word for them. In jail they were visited and revisited by clergymen, lawyers, and assorted busybodies who advised them over and over that, their guilt being clear, a confession was the only hope of avoiding the gallows. The pressure became more than the harried Stephen could stand, and just a few days before the trial was to begin, in the upper room of the jailhouse, he made his written confession.

Yes, wrote Stephen, there had been a quarrel in the Glazier lot that Spring morning. He and Russell Colvin had argued; there had been name-calling; and Russell had walloped him on the shoulder with a stout beech limb. He, in turn, had fetched Russell a back-handed blow on the base of the skull. Russell had fallen and presently had died.

Stephen went on to tell how he had disposed of the body in the cellar hole and tree stump, just as he had been accused of doing.

Almost immediately he was sorry he had written the confession and wanted to retract it, but it was too late.

In those days a murder trial had to be held before the Supreme Court of Vermont, and it was a month before all three members of that body met in Manchester for the Boorn case. So large was the crowd the trial was held in the old Congregational church.

Under laws then in force both a principal and accessory could and did receive similar punishment for a single crime, so both Boorn brothers were tried together, on equal status. Another procedure, forgotten today, provided that an accused person could *not* testify as his own witness or in his own behalf.

Although represented by able counsel, Richard Skinner and Leonard Sargeant, later respectively Governor and Lieutenant-Governor of Vermont, the Boorn boys had to sit silent while the

conflicting tales and opinionated stories they had told years before were dredged up from long memories and used as testimony against them. Most damning, of course, was Stephen's written confession. Lewis Colvin, Russell's young son, testified that he had seen his father and Stephen Boorn beating each other with a stick in the Glazier lot, and, being afraid, he had run home. Stephen had warned him repeatedly not to mention this fact, but he now did so.

So overwhelming was the evidence that, while only a toenail remained to show there had ever been a Russell Colvin, the defense did not even suggest it might well have been someone else's toenail. Since neither defendant could give evidence, their confessions could not and were not denied. The jury had little choice, and found the Boorn brothers guilty of murder. Chief Justice Dudley Chase sentenced them to be hanged on the 28th of the following January. The crowd of six-hundred which had attended the trial went away satisfied that justice had been done.

There was an appeal, of course, which was acted upon by vote of the entire Vermont legislature. They upheld Stephen's sentence by more than two to one, but commuted Jesse's to life imprisonment at the State's Prison in Windsor. Stephen Boorn, hope nearly gone, mumbled dejectedly: "I suppose I must die."

The convicted murderer's chief friend and visitor during these dark days was the Reverend Lemuel Haynes, the respected Manchester pastor. The Reverend Mr. Haynes began life in Connecticut as an abandoned "bond boy" of mixed white and Negro blood. After serving in the Revolution at Ticonderoga, he educated himself and became an ordained minister. He served West Rutland's and Manchester's all-white congregations for over thirty years. The ministrations of this brilliant and selfless man kept the wretched Stephen Boorn in the realm of sanity.

Chained alone to the floor of his gloomy cell, the condemned man read his Bible by candlelight and prayed. People from as far away as Pownal and Brandon already were planning a trek to Manchester in January to see him hanged. The gallows were to be erected next to the whipping post, where Manchester's present courthouse, built in 1822, now stands.

Unknown to Stephen events involving tremendous luck and

amazing coincidence were taking place. In late November two men, total strangers, stood in the lobby of a New York hotel, listening, as was the custom, to the reading aloud of a copy of the *Evening Post*. One man was James Whelpley, formerly a Manchester storekeeper. When an item about the Boorn case and Russell Colvin was read, Whelpley spoke up and told the group of his former acquaintance with Colvin, relating stories about him, his peculiarities and his wanderlust.

Another man in the hotel lobby, Taber Chadwick, listened at first with only half an ear, then more and more intently. Five years before, out in Dover, New Jersey, a relative of his had engaged a hired man, just such a person as Whelpley was describing. The man had called himself "Russell Colvin of Manchester, Vermont." Chadwick lost no time in visiting Dover. Then he sat down and wrote a letter to the New York paper concerning his suspicions.

Mr. Whelpley, fortunately, saw Chadwick's letter when it was published, and he hurried over to New Jersey to see this "Colvin" for himself. Although the plump blond man he found was laboring under many delusions, his looks and familiarity with people and places in Manchester were enough to convince Whelpley that he was indeed Russell Colvin.

Then came the difficult task of persuading Colvin to return to Vermont, something he had no intention of doing. A ruse, involving a lady, got him as far as New York. Next Whelpley convinced him that theWar of 1812 was still on, and that British ships in the harbor necessitated a roundabout detour to New Jersey. It was roundabout, all right: some two-hundred miles due north.

In Manchester the news began to filter through from letters and newspaper articles, but at first there were few who believed it. "It's just someone who looks like Russell," people declared.

But excitement grew as the stages brought Colvin and Whelpley closer to Manchester. In Bennington their arrival emptied an entire courtroom where a hearing had been in session. A stentorian-voiced messenger preceded the coach through Shaftsbury and Arlington. The rutted, snow-blown road was lined with farm people come to see the dead man returned to life.

As the excited horses pranced along the main street of Man-

chester and drew up in front of Captain Black's tavern, the crowd
went wild. Those who had doubted were convinced when they
actually saw Colvin. He, in turn, stood waving his hat and calling
many of them by name.

They took Russell to the jail and found Stephen nearly prostrate
with relief. For once he was very glad to see his brother-in-law.
Russell seemed to have a blank spot in his memory when it came
to his relatives and things concerning them. He innocently asked
why Boorn was in chains.

"Because they say I murdered you!"

"Pshaw," said Colvin, "you never hurt me. Jesse hit me with a
briar once, but it didn't hurt much."

Manchester people, quick to forgive and forget, decided that it
was much better to declare an impromptu holiday right now, two
days before Christmas, than to wait for a solemn hanging in
January. The jailer struck off Stephen's fetters, and he was allowed
to touch off the first of fifty cannon shots fired in honor of the
gala occasion. The next step was to send a delegation over the

mountains to Windsor in order to effect Jesse Boorn's release from prison.

Of course Colvin was subjected to a thorough grilling by the State's Attorney and a battery of sheriff's deputies. He came through with flying colors, and for a few days was lionized wherever he chose to walk about town. Perhaps he recalled the ill-prepared woodchuck dinner, for he refused to have anything to do with his wife.

The real savior of Stephen Boorn, James Whelpley, soon took his often-addled Russell "home" to New Jersey. Later the state paid him in full for his modest expenses in bringing the wanderer back to Vermont.

So ended the Colvin "murder" case. Russell lived out his deluded days in Dover, and the Boorn brothers, free from suspicion at last, hied themselves to the new Western Reserve region of Ohio.

Lawyers and amateur criminologists have been arguing ever since about the strangest aspect of this unusual case. Why did Stephen Boorn confess to a crime he did not commit?

Jesse Boorn's part may be accounted for by fear, and the fact that he saw or participated in a fight. He may well have got in a good lick himself, as Colvin later stated, and perhaps presumed that Colvin had gone off on the mountain to die. By implicating the absent Stephen he was diverting suspicion from himself.

That the personally written confession by Stephen was obtained without duress, is harder to explain. It probably had to do with the fact that he believed the evidence would most certainly convict him. If he confessed, with self-defense carefully pointed out, he might be given life imprisonment instead of death.

Although there was no *corpus delicti* proven in this case, the jury and judge had every reason to arrive at its verdict and sentence, in view of the signed confession. Nobody profited from the affair, except in experience. Laws in Vermont have long since been changed so that there can never be a repetition of such a chain of events.

Barney Boorn's house still stands near Manchester Depot. With a bit of inquiry you can find the old Glazier lot and the shallow depression which marks the site of the cellar hole, where Russell Colvin supposedly was placed "where potatoes wouldn't freeze."

Today one might consider the Boorn-Colvin case a period comedy of errors. But to Stephen Boorn it was far from comic. For a while he stood in the very shadow of the gallows, a victim of what was nearly an appalling miscarriage of justice, in Vermont's most famous mystery.

The Strange Wedding of the Widow Ward

NOEL C. STEVENSON & MURRAY HOYT

OBEDIAH MARTIN, A LAWYER, tells us that on February 22, 1789, in Newfane, Vermont, the widow Hannah Ward, the most beautiful woman in the whole town, married Major Moses Joy. A large gathering watched every instant of the ceremony with rapt attention. Every eye was fixed on the wedding couple; those present seemed especially interested in the gorgeously attractive bride.

Perhaps this was because she had, for the ceremony, laid aside all her clothing.

But we are getting ahead of the story.

Obediah became involved in the matter because he was a friend of Major Joy and wanted to save the good Major from financial ruin and a long jail term. And because the elements of law involved were very interesting to him as a lawyer. His own involvement was what caused him to keep such a complete record of the chronology of events.

Lawyer Martin found Major Joy in his outer office one morning, and they retired to the privacy of the inner room. After they were seated, the good Major licked his lips repeatedly, turned his hat around and around in his hands, and then said, "Obediah, I've got trouble."

Obediah, who must have had an intimate knowledge of Newfane goings-on said, "Widow Hannah Ward?"

The Major looked startled and taken aback. He said, "How did you know?" Obediah only made a superior little lawyers-know-everything gesture with his hand, and smiled an inscrutable smile.

Major Joy said, "I didn't think anybody had the slightest idea I was even courting her." Then he added, "Obediah, what's this law about a new husband becoming liable for a dead husband's debts?"

"*Executor de son tort?*"

"Exe — exec — You don't say! Is that the one where I could become liable for William Ward's debts if I married Hannah Ward?"

"That's the one, Moses. It —"

Moses's hands opened and closed. He almost hitched himself off the front of the chair. His face became softer, his eyes sparkled.

He said with tremendous earnestness, "Obediah, I love that woman. More than anything else I ever wanted, I want to marry Hannah Ward. I can't sleep good at night any more. I can't work good daytimes. I can't —"

"A very natural biological phenom —"

"— stand it to be away from her or wait to get back to her again. I can't —" A look of dismay spread across his face. The animation left it and was replaced with nervous self-consciousness. He muttered, "I guess you'll think I'm silly to —"

"Not silly. A reasonable —"

"But I just *can't* pay William Ward's debts. Why that handsome no-good owed everybody and everybody's little brother. He owed folks clear to Boston. Yes, by George, clear to Albany. How does this exec thing — this law work?"

"Well, literally it means, 'executor of his own wrong.' You see, in common law the husband owns all of his wife's personal possessions, and of course that includes her clothing."

"He can't own that now. He's dead."

"But there has never been a distribution of any part of the estate to her. Her possessions, therefore, are still owned by the estate. The estate is insolvent. As you say, creditors from here to there and back, are roosting in trees like vultures waiting to swoop down on anything valuable under any pretext. Oh, they aren't going to attach a couple of second-hand dresses and some —" he glanced apprehensively at Moses Joy and then finished delicately "— some other things. But if anything was much more valuable than used clothing, they'd swoop."

"But how can they swoop on *me?*"

"Under *executor de son tort*, anybody who meddles with the goods of a deceased person becomes liable for that person's debts."

"All of them? All that mess of —"

116

"All of them. If you married Widow Ward while she was wearing clothes furnished by her late husband, you would be trying to take over, or be 'meddling with', part of his estate. And you would under this law become liable for all his debts."

At first all was gloom. Then suddenly a look of vast relief spread across Major Joy's face.

He said, "Well, we can get around that easy enough. I'll buy her a whole new outfit to be married in. I'll get a dressmaker in Bennington. No, by George, I'll buy the best in all Boston so that —"

"No good. If you married her in clothes furnished by you, which she put on while she was still, so to speak, a part of William Ward, the clothes would be considered a gift by you to the estate, not to her. You'd still be 'meddling' when you got them back by marriage, and you'd be liable. It's common knowledge that you're well-off. Do you honestly believe a single creditor would be fair-minded enough to forgo such a heaven-sent opportunity?"

"No-o-o-o. One or two, maybe. But when you put it that way, not many. And there wouldn't be enough money, well-to-do or not, to cover all that crafty promoter's defaulting schemes."

"Well, if there wasn't, once they obtained a judgment, they could have you thrown into prison under Vermont's debtor's law. You could be there for years, ruined and locked up. Moses, hard as it may seem to you, you've got to give up the idea of marrying this woman."

"But life wouldn't be *worth* living without her. I *won't* live without her."

"What sort of life would it be with you married, in a debtor's prison, and Widow Ward outside? Certainly *that's* not as good as your life right now. No, Moses, you can't fight this; there's no way out; it's too big —"

His voice trailed to a stop because he had the distinct feeling that Major Moses Joy wasn't listening to him any longer. The Major's eyes held a squinting, calculating, far away look.

Then suddenly Major Joy galvanized into action. He jumped to his feet and stretched out his hand to Lawyer Martin.

"Thank you very much," he said, "for warning me. I'll take

117

your advice and make sure I don't pay his debts or land in jail. Thank you."

"Good. I know it's hard to put aside the thought of marrying anyone so lovely, so —"

"Oh, I haven't put that idea aside even for a moment. I'm just not going to pay those debts or go to prison."

"But — but —"

He was still sputtering when the door closed behind the Major.

In the days which followed, Lawyer Obediah Martin heard much on all sides about the plans for Major Joy's wedding. When the exact date was finally settled, he stopped the Major.

He said, "Moses, somehow I haven't gotten across to you how real your danger is if you should go through with this. You seem to feel that nothing can happen to you. It can, and it will. Everybody who understands the true situation is deathly afraid of that law. The courts without exception uphold it. It is a fearsome thing; it can bankrupt the rich and cause the poor to be imprisoned."

"It's a bad law, Obediah."

"Granted. The way it's now interpreted, it's so bad that I have a feeling the interpretation of our courts may actually be based on a misunderstanding of the principles involved. Vermont is very new. Many magistrates have no real education in the law. I'm positive that someday *executor de son tort* will be interpreted very, very differently. But right now it hangs over you, and these plans of yours, like a sword."

They talked a while longer. The best Obediah could get from Major Moses Joy was a vague mumbling that he had a "sort of plan." And finally they parted, Lawyer Martin shaking his head sadly.

On the morning of the wedding, a sudden blinding thought came to Lawyer Martin. It was, in his mind, like the white light of an explosion. It was such an unthinkable idea that at first he put it from him. But the more he remembered little phrases, small words, in the conversations between himself and the Major, the more horrified he became.

Again he sought out Moses Joy.

"If," he said, "you have some crazy idea of forcing that poor woman to — Of course you *couldn't* be thinking of — She wouldn't be a party to —"

"It would handle the situation, wouldn't it?"

"Why — why, yes, but — but it's unthinkable. The disgrace. What would women everywhere say?"

"Better be sure to come to the wedding. Others — plenty of others — plan to be there; no reason you should miss it. It'll likely be worth seeing."

And the Major hurried away.

Obediah Martin went to the wedding, which was held in the Field Mansion on Newfane Hill. He arrived rather early so as not to miss anything. He assured himself piously that he didn't want to miss anything because the thing he missed might be something with which he could somehow help his old friend.

There was much bustling around. Fine ladies and gentlemen, dressed in their best, moved about, greeted one another. It seemed to Lawyer Martin that the women were acting unusually innocent and demure, and the men were more swashbuckling than usual. Over-all he could feel an anticipation, an extreme excitement he had never noticed before during such an event. It was in every move that was made, every word that was spoken.

Major Joy came in and Obediah heard him whisper to the mansion's owner, "Are you sure the room is warm enough? Under the circumstances we must have it much warmer than usual."

Why, the Major must actually be going through with it! Lawyer Martin's heart seemed to drop, then skyrocket into his throat where it remained for an agonizing period. Everyone waited. The room became quiet.

Moses Joy came in and took his place against the far wall. Reverend Hezekial Taylor — known to all as the jolliest parson in the Republic of Vermont — came in and took his place beside the Major. Every eye was on the door; the tension seemed to Obediah almost unbearable.

Then there was a rustling in the hallway and the Widow Ward came forward into the room with her attendants. She was very beautiful, a little pale. A demure little half-smile played around the corners of her mouth.

Well, at least she was still clothed. But what clothing! It was in almost fantastic contrast to the beautiful silks worn by her attendants. Obediah could hear a little gasp as people got their first glimpse of it.

The clothes were shabby and old. Terribly shabby. They weren't, and never had been, wedding clothes. The threadbare old dress and the jacket, in their very best days, couldn't have been labeled a "gown." And certainly there was no train, no veil.

She stopped near the Major, the demure half-smile on her lips more pronounced now. Very slowly she unfastened the small jacket.

She unfastened the buttons one at a time. She slowly removed the garment. She held it out in front of her between her thumb and first finger. For several moments she stood there, and there was no sound but the breathing of the guests. Then she dropped it in a heap on the floor.

Lawyer Martin thought, "She's going to do it. I — I didn't believe she would. O dear! This is terrible!"

For a moment longer she stood there. Then she moved forward, followed by one of her attendants. She went to the door of a closet in the far wall.

She opened the closet and stood for a second in the doorway for a last look at those assembled. Then she and the attendant moved across the closet threshold and closed the door behind them.

For the first time Obediah Martin really looked at that closet door. It was like any other door in the room except that there was a heart-shaped hole, which looked newly cut, in its exact center.

There was a rustling inside, and what might even have been a subdued giggle or two.

Then the door opened again, this time only enough to allow the attendant to come out into the main room. She carried with her a pile of clothing; the shabby dress the Widow Ward had worn,

and on top of that, stockings and other items which caused a little feminine gasp to rise from the guests. It was easy to see that everything she had worn was on that pile. There was much dainty turning away of feminine heads.

The attendant placed the pile of clothing atop the jacket on the floor, then stepped over against the closet door.

Then through the heart-shaped hole in the door a graceful hand was extended. Next an incredibly white, rounded, lovely, and very feminine arm came into view. The Major reached for the hand with the fervor of a youth, held it in his. He looked up then and faced Reverand Taylor.

Reverend Taylor cleared his throat and began, "Dearly Beloved, we — ." Thus was the naked widow, standing in the darkened closet, married to Moses Joy.

When the ceremony was over another attendant appeared carrying a pile of lovely silk. She went to the closet door, passed inside.

In a short time the elegantly attired Widow Ward, now Mrs. Moses Joy, came out, her smile radiant. She was kissed hard by the eager Major, then standing hand in hand with him, received the congratulations of her friends.

Obediah Martin was one of the most effusive of the congratulators, and there was definite relief in his whole bearing. But it was peculiar that he found himself unable completely to suppress a sense of disappointment, of letdown. Certainly he had no idea from what *that* feeling could have stemmed.

And so Obediah's friends, Major and Mrs. Joy, just as fictional stories ended in those days, lived happily (and financially secure) ever after.

The Money Diggers

STEPHEN GREENE

TREASURE HUNTING, WHICH HAS FLOURISHED FOR CENTURIES, is a comfortingly constant phenomenon in a changing world. Although the magic stone and divining rod of the treasure hunter have come to be supplemented (but not supplanted) by the mine detector, the geophone, and the scintillation counter, today's seeker has the traditional goals, appetites and faith. He needs his faith, for the ratio of successful treasure hunts to unsuccessful ones cannot be an encouraging figure.

The gold and silver, of course, are there: The known lost and missing treasures today have been valued at $260 billion. This figure is not hard to believe if one remembers that plenty of gold-bearing galleons and other vessels have been lost on island reefs, and that the occasional provident pirate actually did bury his booty against a rainy day. (West Indian natives explain that buccaneers' wealth is seldom found because the spirits that watch over it whisk it away as soon as the hiding place is disturbed.) Enough attempts at finding treasure are successful, followed by wide publicity, to keep the susceptible alert.

Vermont, while an inland state and thus not a regular beat for either galleons or pirates, has nonetheless enjoyed its full share of treasure stories. The area in which most of these tales, and consequently of digging, have occurred during the past two centuries — Vermont's treasure belt, we might call it — stretches north and south pretty well along the Green Mountain range.

Here, local histories record, some twenty-seven towns have been tantalized by tales of underground fortunes of gold, silver or jewels that have found their way into our granite and notably non-jewel-bearing hills, usually by human agency, and which are now

123

practically lying there for the taking. In many, if not most cases digging has resulted — in some places quite an impressive amount of digging. The results to date have been meager.

Bristol is a case in point. It lies not far from the center of the state. Here, just south of the village, at the foot of a ragged west-facing cliff (said to be a rare Vermont habitat of the rattlesnake), digging started in the early 1800's and has continued with varying degrees of enthusiasm ever since.

Bristol is not necessarily the most important of Green Mountain treasure sites. It is much the best-known one, however, because of the interest of a talented local chronicler, an amateur historian named Franklin Stephen Harvey who was born in Bristol not a mile from the scene of our story, and who lived there off and on all his life. With an instinct for the dramatic and an eye for detail, he wrote in 1888 and 1889 a series of articles for the *Bristol Herald* telling of the peculiar goings-on in his hometown. His lively account has proved a happy hunting ground for nonfiction writers ever since.

It all started, according to Mr. Harvey, back in 1800. Bristol, then known as Pocock, was pioneer country and its inhabitants were few. One day, at what served as a store in those times, appeared a "rough and uncanny" stranger with a foreign accent, a reticent old man who bought some eatables and straight-way disappeared. It was later that some boys found him digging among the rocks at the foot of the gloomy cliff on South Mountain; and only later still could he be persuaded, by a threat to move him off as a trespasser, to tell what he was about.

His name, he finally admitted, was DeGrau. He was Spanish. Many years earlier his father, a miner, had traveled this county with a party of countrymen in search of precious metals, and in Bristol they had discovered a rich vein of silver. The men went away to procure the necessary mining equipment and returned the next year, this time with one or two women and young DeGrau in tow. Once at work, their success was gratifying: The ore proved to be rich, the vein extensive, and the industry of the miners was rewarded by an immense treasure smelted into silver bars. By Fall, when ready to return home, they found they could carry with them only a small portion of their riches. The bulk of

125

it, together with the tools, was walled up in a cave shaped like an old-fashioned brick oven and so covered with earth and moss that it would be indistinguishable for what it was to the passer-by. Then the men went back to their distant homes, agreeing to meet the following Summer to pick up the balance of their silver. But on no account, they agreed, was any of the party to return without the others. The years rolled by as one thing after another prevented their coming. One by one the others died, until DeGrau remained the sole survivor. Now he had returned, he told his audience, for the silver that was all his.

This was the substance of the Spaniard's story. On the whole, the residents of Pocock believed him. Mr. Harvey writes that he had talked to several of the men who had known DeGrau, and the Spaniard appeared to them neither an imposter nor a mental case.

Moreover there were details in his story that made good sense to his audience. The old man told, for example, of going as a boy to the river a mile and a half away and cutting alder to burn into charcoal for use in the mining operations. And he said that when one of the woman members of the party had died, they had sunk her body in a pond a hundred yards west of the diggings to prevent the wolves from getting her. It all, the witnesses said, had the ring of truth.

But if the treasure was buried in Bristol, DeGrau couldn't find it. He said that the face of the mountain seemed to have changed since his boyhood and that it was barely possible that he was looking in the wrong spot. Still he didn't think so: There were landmarks that made him believe he was on the right track. So he pushed boulders around, dug some holes in the unresponsive ledge, and finally disappeared and was never seen again.

DeGrau was the first in a procession that almost certainly has not yet ended. Next to dig were some of the residents of Pocock, who started in where DeGrau had left off. As luck would have it, someone found under a rock, where it had obviously lain for years, an antique vessel of strange design about the size of a quart measure. The money diggers — a misnomer, it has been pointed out, in the case of this story because silver metal and not money was involved, but a favorite appellation for Vermont treasure hunters — were sure it was a crucible left by the Spaniards.

Others thought that it must have been something left by the Indians. Wherever it came from, its discovery gave new stimulus to the digging. People now came from far and near to pry away the loose rocks and to do some scratching at the foot of the cliff. One Richard Brown, a local man, worked here part of each Spring and Fall until his death, appearing and disappearing again as regularly, Mr. Harvey says, as the north and south flights of the migrating goose.

Up to now the digging had been done for the most part by men working alone. In 1840, however, half a dozen middle-aged and elderly Canadians appeared in Bristol; they were joined by others, a stock company was organized — and the real boom was under way. The guiding spirit of the Canadian group was Simeon Coreser, a heavy-featured, yellow-haired, red-faced giant of a man of about sixty years of age, with little education but with a fund of good stories and a personality that both repelled and fascinated young Harvey. He would hide in the rocks when he saw the youth coming and growl like a bear, and his stories of phantom dogs and bleeding boys were chilling. Uncle Sim, as they called him, did none of the actual work, claiming incapacity by virtue of a hernia, but acted as a sort of director of operations. He kept in touch with the fortune-tellers who told the Canadians where to dig; he gained converts to the cause and raised funds. This last was done with a promise that every dollar invested — whether as food for

127

the diggers, or credit at the store, or, best of all, cash — would bring the investor a hundred dollars when the treasure was found.

One shaft after another was sunk into the rock, where the walls were damp and the air cold. One of these shafts, Harvey writes, was still open when the historian was recording the story. It was the most westerly one, and led down into the solid rock in an almost perpendicular direction for forty or fifty feet. It then took an abrupt horizontal turn and led off for more than a hundred feet right under the base of the mountain. "There are three other excavations between that and the mountain, all of them within a few yards of each other, and all reaching down to a far greater depth than the one just described. One of them, after more than a hundred feet of sheer descent, also starts off under the mountain" and leads some one hundred and fifty feet away in a northeasterly direction. "For half an acre all around, the surface is literally honeycombed with holes a few feet in depth, where generation after generation of money diggers have worked their superstitious energies on this solid ledge."

The Bristol diggers put in days, weeks and months of back-breaking work in Hell's Half Acre, as it came to be called, and the only excitement was a series of bitter crises. One shaft had to be abandoned because of "foul air" after it had gone down more than seventy feet. (Harvey watched them light a torch of white-birch bark, saturated with turpentine, and saw it suddenly snuffed out when it had been lowered to a certain depth.) Winter storms plugged the shaft entrances, and Spring thaws flooded the tunnels with water. At first the water was laboriously bucketed out by hand, a time-consuming job. When a pump was secured, grit in the water cut out the valves.

Finally someone suggested a syphon, and Harvey comments that it is ironic that the men grumbled over the investment required for lead pipe for the syphon. They willingly swallowed traditional wild stories, but were skeptical of the efficacy of making water run uphill.

It was only after twelve years' work and an investment of about ten thousand dollars that Uncle Sim and his group grew discouraged and went home. Then ten years later, in 1860, Coreser was back again, ragged and shaking with palsy, to work the diggings alone. A fortune-teller had revealed, he said, that by removing a few rocks a passage could be opened leading directly to the treasure cave. The Canadian feebly poked and pried into the rocks for two months, then he too disappeared.

"Have a little charity for those misguided men, all of you who can," Harvey writes in conclusion. "In pounding those rocks, they injured no one but themselves. Who will say that that is not a great improvement on the bloody record of the Salem witchcraft."

But that is not the end of the search. In the 1930's another determined effort was made to find the DeGrau treasure. The digging is probably going on in Bristol today, as you read these words. It was, in any case, still a tale of romantic appeal a century or so ago when Daniel Pierce Thompson, the Vermont novelist, made it the subject of more than one of his romances. The best known *May Martin, or The Money Diggers*, went through at least fifty editions (many of them pirated) and was made into a play and shown on the stage of the Boston Museum in 1846.

What is even stranger than the DeGrau story itself is that the same narrative, varying only in detail, crops up in the history of at least a score of other Vermont towns, each of which claims the returning Spaniard, and the buried trove, as its own.

For example, a Chester man relates that when young he had done a favor to an old man passing through his hometown on horseback. The aged horseman, in return, told the same yarn we have just heard ascribed to DeGrau. But in the Chester version the saddlebags of the old man are bulging with silver. He had found the mine again, in this case in the "white rocks" two miles east of North Wallingford village.

In Brandon, the account is again substantially the same as Bristol's, but here the men were driven away by hostile Indians; as indeed they were in the Huntington version of the story.

In most of these variations on what we may call the Bristol/De-Grau theme, the group is described as "Spaniards," but some town histories call them "explorers," others "counterfeiters" — and in one case "Bostonians." (The Bostonians, in thrifty Boston style, were taking their fortune north to invest with the enterprising Allen brothers.) It is usually silver coin or silver bars that the miners hide, but also interred are jewels, golden bars, golden

ducats, and golden watches "preserved in sweet oil." At times these treasures are said to have been mined on the spot (although the State Geologist today says that Vermont can boast no true silver and precious little gold), and at other times the men are carrying it north (or sometimes south) through the state. In one case, on the side of Camel's Hump they are manufacturing it, for some reason unexplained, into Spanish coin.

The appeal of the DeGrau theme is shown by the fact that it has found congenial soil not only in 10 percent of Vermont's communities, but in other areas as well. Practically every state in the West has its lost-mine story, although most do not follow the Bristol/DeGrau line. Peter Fleming, in one of his absorbing true-adventure stories, tells of a group of Spaniards who bury their treasure when pursued; when all but one of the group has died, the survivor returns to attempt to find it. The locale of the Fleming story is the coast of Brazil.

DeGrau, although the archetype for the Green Mountains, is not the only hero of treasure folklore: Captain Kidd plays a role too.

This luckless Scottish ship's captain was hanged and gibbeted in 1701 ostensibly for knocking down and killing a mutinous crew member. Of course this was then considered reasonably correct behavior in a ship's captain, but in actuality Kidd was being made the scapegoat for an embarrassed British administration. On returning from a cruise to the Indian Ocean, he had buried some treasure on Gardiner Island, in Long Island Sound, but it was dug up again by order of the authorities. Although this is the only buried loot with which Kidd can be associated, after more than two hundred and fifty years his treasure is still being sought in a wide variety of unlikely sites. Kidd never got much farther inland than his own comfortable home on Liberty Street in New York City, but three Vermont towns — Waitsfield, Middlesex, and Bellows Falls — have been combed for his treasure, and the Wallingford trove referred to above has been ascribed to him, as well as to the ubiquitous Spaniards.

Other sources of treasure legends in Vermont include the raid by Robert Rogers and his Rangers on the Indian village of St. François de Sales in 1759 (see *Vermont Life*, Autumn 1952). And following Burgoyne's surrender at Saratoga, his paymaster is supposed to have disappeared with the pay of the defeated troops — a story of understandable appeal in neighboring Bennington County.

Almost any semiplausible report, really, can be made the excuse for a good treasure hunt. The human love of easy money, or what its followers hope will be easy money, goes back as long as written history and explains endless quests for the gold at the foot of the rainbow. A half-century and more before DeGrau showed up in Bristol, Benjamin Franklin was writing in his Busy-Body paper No. 8:

... There are among us great numbers of honest artificers and laboring people, who, fed with a vain hope of growing suddenly rich, neglect their business, almost to the ruining of themselves and families, and voluntarily endure abundance of fatigue in a fruitless search after imaginary hidden treasure. They wander through the woods and bushes by day, to discover the marks and signs; at midnight they repair to the hopeful spots with spades and pick-axes; full of expectation, they labor violently, trembling at the same time in every joint, through fear of certain malicious demons, who are said to haunt and guard such places. At length a mighty hole is dug, and perhaps several cart-loads of earth thrown out; but, alas, no keg or iron pot is found! No seaman's chest crammed with Spanish pistoles, or weighty pieces of eight! Then they conclude, that, through some mistake in the procedure, some rash word spoke, or some rule of art neglected, the guardian spirit had power to sink it deeper into the earth, and convey it out of their reach. Yet, when a man is once thus infatuated, he is so far from being discouraged by ill success, that he is rather animated to double his industry, and will try again and again in a hundred different places, in hopes at last of meeting with some lucky hit, that shall at once sufficiently reward him for all his expense of time and labor.

The colonists were great tellers of tales. "The habit of story-telling," writes folklore authority Richard M. Dorson, "took early root in colonial New England. Pioneer families crowded around the hearth fire at the close of the day entertained themselves with tales of mystery and marvel, begotten from the actual scenes in their wilderness life upon which inherited fancies were easily grafted. In all the New England states the custom is recorded; lacking books, loving horrors, bred in demonology, and surrounded by dread animals and savages, colonial Americans turned naturally into vivid spinners and eager consumers of folkyarn. Cradled and nurtured in the wonder-laden atmosphere of a new world and stimulated by a brimstone theology that clothed evil in human form, this native flair for storytelling found continuous expression and ready opportunity with the nation's growth."

The newspapers of the day bear witness to frontier interest in accidental deaths, weird natural happenings, miracles, murders, ghosts and witches. In fact, witches were then universal (and lest we get the idea that they departed the scene after Salem, Bergen Evans points out in his *Natural History of Nonsense* that *The New York Times* in the decade after 1862 carried stories of more than fifty cases of witchcraft; furthermore, Evans believes that in the mid-Twentieth Century the majority of the people of the world believed in witchcraft).

A couple of centuries ago, men raised to prominence and considered levelheaded were not immune from superstition. Huckleberry Finn's notions were fairly tame compared with those recorded by Thurlow Weed, New York journalist and politician, who recalled a boyhood excursion around 1810 to dig gold in the moonlight, when "the throat of a black cat was cut and the precise spot was indicated by the direction the blood spurted." In Vermont a generation earlier, Silas Hamilton — selectman, town representative, and large landowner in Whitingham — gave the following "method to Tak up hid Treasure" in a diary he kept during the 1780's, with all entries devoted to treasure hunting:

Tak Nine Steel Rods about ten or twelve Inches in Length Sharp or Piked to Perce in to the Erth, and let them be Besmeared with fresh blood from a hen mixed with hogdung. Then mak two Surkels Round the hid Treasure one of Sd Surkels a Littel Larger in surcumference than the hid Treasure lays in the Erth the other Surkel Sum Larger still, and as the hid treasure is wont to move to North or South East or west Place your Rods as is Discribed on the other sid of this leaf.

Upstate in Braintree, scythes rather than rods were used to contain the always elusive trove. It was just about to be dug up, we are told in one account, when an envious bystander pulled

one of the scythes out of the ground and the pot of money escaped through the opening. One witness distinctly saw the ground rise and sink, as if dislodged by a mole, in the path of the moving pot.

There are no conscious liars among the tellers of treasure tales, declared such an authority on the subject as Ralph D. Paine; the spell is upon them. They believe their own yarns, and they prove their faith by back-breaking work with pick and shovel.

So it is with Vermonters, to whom these sentiments are notably applicable, for the Green Mountains are a last frontier of the pioneer spirit, and the natives aren't afraid of a lick of work.

True, hereabouts the returns on effort, as we have pointed out, so far have been especially thin. The only more or less authenticated success story in local money digging annals concerns treasure not located in the state at all: An old chest found in an attic in Middlesex, near Montpelier, contained the clue to a $20,000 cache buried on the coast of Maine. There is also the account, highly suspect, it should be said, in an old *Poultney Journal* of three Fair Haven hunters who ran on to a cave containing an iron kettle, some Spanish gold, 1,530 rattlesnakes lying torpid in a pile, and five "grinning" human skeletons. The gold proved to be worth $2,750 and the bounty on half a bushel of rattles yielded a further $1,765.

None of which affects DeGrau's treasure, which waits, quite safe, for someone with the will and the luck to find it. Or to find a forgotten hoard of Captain Kidd's. If you're treasure minded, and roaming around up here, you'll run into Vermonters who know positively of these or other buried fortunes. And it's possible they'll cut you in for a slice of the loot if you'll just stake them for a month or two.

Odd Men Out

LESLIE C. MOORE

VERMONTERS HAVE USUALLY BEEN REGARDED BY OUTSIDERS as standing somewhat apart from the rest of Americans. But within the state, people occasionally come along whom even Vermonters have to think of as standing outside the usual run of humanity.

They are people like the man who invented the cowcatcher because he felt sorry for cows, the man who refused to touch anything anyone else had touched, and the man who insisted on attending the state legislature as the representative of a town that did not exist. They are the eccentrics, the people who are faithful to singular ideals, who have a vision of the world unique to themselves, and who are prepared to live by their own standards at whatever cost to themselves.

The true eccentric is unique by definition. Nobody else can share his particular faith to the extent that he does, or in just the same way.

If he founds a religion, it must fail. William Miller of New Haven, Vermont, is a splendid example. He predicted, on the basis of prophecies in the Book of Daniel, that the world would come to an end between April 21, 1843 and April 21, 1844. When nothing happened, a disciple suggested October 22, 1844. By this time the numbers of faithful spread over the eastern United States were slipping from their 1843 high of 50,000, and after October 22 the figure became a handful, who evolved into Seventh-Day Adventists. Miller died in 1849, still confident that Judgment Day was just a few years away.

The career of Benoni Wright, of Bradford, was even briefer. He retired to a cave on what is now called Wright's Mountain to fast and prepare himself to be a prophet of the Lord. He let his beard grow, and he wore a belt with forty-two holes. He intended to take his belt in a notch a day as he grew thinner. Three weeks later he was found one night searching for food at a farm and his spiritual career was ended.

Secular eccentrics are less known, but equally interesting. For instance, Orson Clement of West Corinth merely seemed to have been a somewhat miserly sheep farmer. He never bought a newspaper, his hired man and his housekeeper lived on scraps, and his one cow, "so old she could have voted," was milked only as a cup or pitcherful was needed.

Then a few other clues about his character appear. He did not think it proper to ask the hired man to ride into town with him, but if the man got into the carriage while his back was turned, he could take him along in all decency. He could not bear to pay taxes, so he would let the sheriff seize the horses he raised, then follow him into town and buy them back at the sale.

In 1870 he inherited his father's six-hundred-acre farm and several hundred pounds of wool which his father had bought at a dollar a pound as a speculation. Orson went on raising sheep for some years, but he refused to sell any of his wool. The price of wool had been dropping every year since the Civil War as large Western sheep ranches opened up and the railroads made it easier to bring the wool east. So, as every shearing time passed, more wool was stored on Orson's farm. It went into the barn until the stalls, the bridle room and the loft were filled. Then it went into the granary until that was filled. And then it went into the house until several rooms there were filled.

Orson no doubt would have died amidst all his wool, but salvation appeared at Sarajevo in 1914. As the United States began selling wool to combatant countries and then started manufacturing woolen uniforms for its own army, the price of wool soared. Yet Orson did not look on World War I as salvation. He had saved his wool for so long that now he *could not* sell it. Perhaps he had set some imaginary, impossibly high price for it. Perhaps he just could not bear to part with it. At any rate the Federal government decided it needed the wool, and in 1918 it seized it. Current market prices were paid, and Orson made $30,000.

So much for that, thought his neighbors in Corinth. But Orson had fooled them all. In 1922 he died, and they found, locked in the granary basement and hidden under hay in the barn, thousands of pounds of wool that he had kept back from the government confiscators.

After his death most of his money went to Dartmouth College, but a thousand dollars went to Mrs. Bradbury, his housekeeper. Once, after a quarrel with her, Orson had cut his will into pieces. Later on he made up with her, but a new will was never written. After his death the pieces of the old one were found, fitted together, and admitted to probate.

Orson Clement was a success, but most eccentrics are not. More typical of those who were in business fields was one of Orson's townsmen, Daniel Flagg.

In the 1830's and '40's, when railroads were just beginning to spread across the country, no provisions had yet been made for keeping animals off the tracks. Daniel was already known as an animal lover — he refused to wear shoes because they were made out of cowhide — and this new hazard obviously cried for redress.

The one cowcatcher in the country was on the locomotive *John*

137

Bull and had been devised by the chief engineer of the New Jersey railroad company that owned it. It was not much—a low bar at right angles to the tracks—but it was a considerable improvement over the first cowcatcher which was two iron prongs riding on a small truck in front of the engine. A few days after *that* was introduced on the line, it hit a charging bull, and the animal had to be pulled off with a block and tackle. But even the newer horizontal bar gave a beast quite a jolt.

It required a man of nobler spirits and compassion, a Daniel Flagg, to think of bending the bar into a prow shape so that the animal would be brushed off to the side and not just battered to pieces.

Daniel showed a model of his idea to a friend one evening. The next day his friend hired a horse and left for Washington to patent the plans for himself. Daniel, of course, followed, and it was now that he gained immortality. He refused to ride a horse, so he walked, and he refused to wear shoes, *so he walked barefoot.*

By the time he got to Washington, the patent had already been given. Officials were convinced of his idea's originality but their hands were tied. In the end, Daniel got a lifetime pass on the railroads, but nothing more.

Some people have too much fun to conform. When the St. Johnsbury meetinghouse was raised in the fall of 1804, Zibe Tute stood on his head on the ridgepole drinking from a whiskey flask. Things like that ran in the family. His sister Sally used to challenge men to bareback horse races up and down St. Johnsbury's Main Street while *she* drank from a flask too. And when a cousin, Jonathan, died of smallpox down in Vernon, near the Massachusetts border, his parents had an inscription put on his tombstone that said in part:

> *Behold the amazing alteration*
> *Effected by inoculation*
> *The means employed his life to save*
> *Hurried him headlong to the grave!*

The town of Corinth seems to have been ripe ground for this sort of people. Horace McDuffee, who lived there in the latter half of the nineteenth century and also was a graduate engineer from Dartmouth, tried to make up for his small size with overalls worn in so many layers that the last one had to be fastened with horse-blanket pins. But he was proud of his appearance, and once had his picture taken to send to Sears, Roebuck.

North of Montpelier, in Calais, lived Pardon Janes, the man who would not touch anything anyone else had touched. As a young man, he was known for his intelligence and his ability as a public speaker. He represented Calais in the state legislature from 1828 to 1831, and before that he had been one of the town selectmen.

But then — apparently sometime in the 1830's — he began, for no known reason, to refuse to handle objects that had touched human flesh, or to touch other flesh himself. He was especially averse to things that women had touched. Until his death in 1870, he carried around a short pitchfork bearing a tin pail on the end of it. He carried money in the pail, and when he had to go to the store, clerks would make change out of the pail for him.

So far as is known, the neighbors of people like Pardon Janes left them alone, newspapers treated their quirks with respect, and no one made it his business to try to have them committed to asylums. Money helped some of them maintain their eccentricities, but others gained the respect of their communities because their strength of character was recognized under the odd behavior to which it had given rise.

In the 1850's in Salisbury, a lawyer named Columbus Smith built a pseudo-Italian mansion and named it "Shard Villa" after a case he had won in London. For forty days in Chancery, he had argued the £80,000 estate of Mary Shard out of the hands of the Crown into those of his client. Supposedly, his hair turned white during this trial, which made his reputation and fortune. The mansion is still Shard Villa, by will a home for "Christian men and temperate women."

At the same time Pardon Janes began serving in the legislature, Ivory Luce was the Representative from Mansfield. The only description we have of him says, "Mr. Luce is well known to many in the State as a man of good natural intellect, and of the most unyielding will, when fully aroused."

In 1849 Mansfield, the town he had represented for thirteen sessions in Montpelier, was dissolved, part merging with Stowe, and part with Underhill. Thirty or forty citizens of the town, dissented, and decided to elect Ivory Luce as their Representative anyway.

On October 11th of that year, the House of Representatives opened its session and Mr. Luce's credentials were questioned. The next day the minutes of the Town Meeting of Mansfield were sent for, to see if the town indeed *had* decided to do away with itself. On October 29th proof came back that the town of Mansfield was no more, and on October 30th Mr. Luce was paid for his attendance and his traveling expenses.

Still not content, he decided to test the Act annexing much of Mansfield to Stowe. So when the sheriff at Stowe tried to seize some of his son's land for nonpayment of taxes, he sued the sheriff for trespassing. He lost, and finally gave up to the inevitable.

In 1902 there was a debate at Montpelier on a Vermont speed limit for automobiles. It was finally fixed at fifteen miles per hour, but the Representative from Middlebury stood up to propose that the loathsome machines be banished from the state entirely.

The man was Joseph Battell, and the range of his enthusiasms, and the individuality of his quirks, put him in a class by himself. His father, Philip, had practiced law in Cleveland, but in 1839, when Joseph was born, he returned to Middlebury, where he had graduated from college. Philip apparently embodied the Protestant ethic and the spirit of capitalism, and he left his son a strict sense of morality and a great deal of money.

Joseph, like his father, started at Middlebury College, but in his junior year he contracted a pulmonary disease that left him with a collapsed lung and a sagging shoulder.

He went abroad in 1861, and on his return three years later published the journal of his travels through France, Italy, and Switzerland. Titled *The Yankee Boy from Home*, it is full of the most routine observations of his trip — until he gets to Chapter Twenty-three.

Chapters Twenty-three to Twenty-six are titled "Whisperings of an Old Pine, 1, 2, 3, and 4." The narrator starts off, "Yes! I am an old Pine, standing on the mountain top. I am very, very old." The story the pine tells is of a girl named Ellen and her younger sister, Bertha. They live in the valley below Lincoln

Mountain where he grows, and they come up to the mountain to tell him of their romances.

The year after *Yankee Boy from Home* was published, Joseph Battell bought the Parker farm in Ripton. He made it into a summer hotel and invited a few friends. The next summer his friends brought *their* friends, and within a few years its informal atmosphere made it a success. Prices varied according to a guest's ability to pay. Battell refused to lose more than two-thousand dollars a year on the place, but he was disappointed when he did not lose at least a few hundred. He named the hotel the Bread Loaf Inn, and the only people who could stay there were those recommended by previous guests.

Battell's iron-bound requirement for all his guests was that they should love nature. If intruders came up the road, Battell would go down to the front of the inn and thunder at them to get out. A lady, watching such an incident from the veranda, remarked of the trespassers, "They probably think this is a lunatic asylum and suppose we are the patients."

His thundering could be impressive. He stood a little under six feet but he was a solidly built two-hundred pounds. He had light brown hair and blue eyes that everyone described as "flashing."

Battell's campaign to preserve Vermont forests eventually became his greatest success. But even then his individual way of doing things showed. He saved the forests by *buying* them. By the time he died his holdings were fantastic, and he was by far the largest landowner in the state. From Monastery Mountain northward forty miles to Camel's Hump, he owned all the land in sight of Bread Loaf Inn. It amounted to over thirty-thousand acres of wilderness woodland.

In 1884 he bought the Middlebury *Register* and began using the newspaper to advertise the Bread Loaf Inn and to encourage more and better breeding of the Morgan horse. Later on his scientific theories and his campaign against the automobile began to take up space of their own. Battell was described as "the most enthusiastic breeder of the Morgan Horse that ever lived," and he compiled and published *The Morgan Horse Register*, a two-volume catalogue and genealogy of every purebred Morgan then known in the country.

Sometime between 1895 and 1900 he had Professor Robert Boyce of Middlebury begin tutoring him on all aspects of arithmetic, algebra and calculus. He was getting ready to begin writing what he considered would be the crowning work of his life. It would be a review of all science and philosophy, and its title would be *Ellen, or the Whisperings of an Old Pine*. In 1901 the work was published, and as Martin Gardner points out in *Fads and Fallacies in the Name of Science*, "Few odder works than *Ellen* have ever appeared in the United States."

As in the story in *Yankee Boy from Home*, the work is a dialogue between the pine tree on Lincoln Mountain and the sixteen-year-old girl, Ellen. But unlike the conversations in that brief story, *Ellen* covers several years and fills two volumes. In all, there are over six hundred pages dedicated to exposing the follies of atheism, deism, evolution, and particularly the wave theories of light and sound. Battell believed that sound was "particles of electrical matter." These, he said, "are introduced into the bodily system, and by their assimilation produce signals which the soul readily interprets.

Battell in his introduction to the work acknowledges his dependence for his scientific knowledge to be primarily on *Chambers' Encyclopaedia* and the *Encyclopaedia Britannica*. But he felt free to set forth his new views as his common sense seemed to dictate. For instance, his theories of algebra:

"But why," I the Old Pine asked, "does Ellen not make her illustrations general by using letters?"

"Because numbers are very much more intelligible," she answered, "and equally general. For whatever is true of one set of numbers, because of the universality of natural law, is true of all sets of numbers similarly used."

"Then," I said, "the oft-repeated remark in text books that letters are better on this account, is not true?"

"Not at all is it true," she replied; "the truth being that they are infinitely inferior, because far less intelligible. It is this same kind of stupidity which has held mathematics back for 2000 years."

Ellen is somewhat less harsh with Newton than with the mathematicians. His blunders, as Ellen thinks, "are mainly due to the mistakes of others and his natural repugnance to disagreeing. Hence his errors on sound, and blundering announcing on the principle of attraction."

It is not clear just what errors Battell found in Newton's theories of gravity, but a clue might be found in his own strange cosmology:

For Ellen thinks that the streams of space are similar to our rivers, only they are a great deal deeper and wider and stronger, as they have to be, for the vessels of the spheres which sail along their courses must needs have a sufficient stream to make their trips in.

Ellen was illustrated with about two-hundred photographs of the scenery around Bread Loaf, all taken by Battell, and most of them featuring pretty girls. Battell never posed for a photograph himself, possibly because of his stooped shoulder, but he loved to take his own camera out on chaperoned drives with the local girls he had selected for models. He would spend hours choosing landscapes for backgrounds, posing the girls against them, and figuring out the light angles and the composition.

A teetotaler, Battell took the only drink of his life to please an acquaintance from Kentucky. Then he found that the Kentuckian would not touch the stuff. In the matter of food, for breakfast Joseph liked lemonade and milk toast.

144

By 1910 Battell's campaign against automobiles was in full swing. A random copy of the *Register* features these headlines: "Two Die in Crash;" "Found under Auto;" "Killed Seeking to Avoid Death;" and "Mother Tries Suicide After Her Boy Is Killed." Many of these stories, along with editorial comments, were assembled into a pamphlet, *Shall Automobiles Have Their Own Roads?* He suggested a network of roads parallel to, but at least four rods from, the roads already existing. He once placed a man with a shotgun on the road leading to the inn to keep out automobiles, but was forced to abandon his roadblock.

Copies of *Ellen* that had been in every guest's room at Bread Loaf, like Gideon Bibles, were still there twenty years after Battell's death in 1915, when the inn had become the Middlebury College Bread Loaf School of English. By then, though, they were serving as casters and doorstops.

Battell was the best so far among those men who for so long a time gave Vermonters the reputation of outspokenness and integrity. He had what is both the eccentric's greatest virtue and his greatest failing — that fixed vision that can only see a goal and the immediate means to it. His example — and the example of the many Vermonters left who are like him — may encourage those who prefer to form their own characters, rather than have society do it for them.

Case of the Rejected Hero

ALTON HALL BLACKINGTON

I HAVE ALWAYS BEEN INTRIGUED BY THE NAMES of certain New England towns. Finding out where these names came from in the first place has been one of my most rewarding hobbies.

Take, for instance, the town of Barton, Vermont, organized on the 28th of March 1798. Few people today realize it was never intended to be called Barton, but behind this lies the amazing story of a brilliant military hero, jailed and forgotten.

It all started shortly after the Revolutionary War drew to a close, when a group of Yankee patriots who had been fighting in Massachusetts and Rhode Island petitioned the independent Republic of Vermont for "a sizeable tract of wild land" which they proposed to clear and establish as a new town, to be known as "Providence." The petition was granted on October 20, 1781. Then, sometime later, it was discovered the town had been named not for the Rhode Island capital — but "Barton."

For a long time no one knew who had tampered with papers and changed the names. Years later it was reported by Abner Allyn of Charleston (perhaps with malicious intent, since he descended from our hero's final nemesis) that one of the original petitioners had whipped out his hunting knife, scratched out the word "Providence" and written in his own name. The town, at any rate, has been "Barton" ever since.

This enterprising chap was William Barton from Rhode Island, where a few years earlier he had, almost singlehandedly, captured the British commander, Richard Prescott, at Newport.

Two of Barton's associates in the new town, equally audacious and better known, were Ira Allen, brother of Ethan, and John Paul Jones, neither of whom took part in the actual settlement. It

147

was not until 1795 that the first settlers reached Barton, bringing all their goods on horseback, a prodigious task. The first route to be hacked through this wilderness ran from the Hazen Military Road at Greensboro through Glover and on to Barton. It was hardly more than a trail. Felled trees served as corduroy fill and primitive bridges were placed over rushing streams. Soon a few mills were put up along the Barton River and a scattering of rough shelters were built.

Barton's cabin was rough indeed, having neither chimney, wood floor nor windows. He cleared three or four acres and cut ten more, in 1795 raising forty bushels of wheat. In the summer of 1796 he constructed the first sawmill in town. Barton helped erect a big log house which was used both as school and church. He was one of a three-man committee which laid out the town's lots.

Unlike most of the first settlers, William Barton never did send for his family. His wife and children remained in Rhode Island, and thus one assumes his interest in the new town was purely speculative. When the first Town Meeting was held in 1798 he took no part, did not vote. Selling of timber and lots seemed his main interests.

This was the activity which brought Barton to trouble. It began in 1797 when a lot he had sold to Solomon Wadhams of Brookfield turned out to be owned by another. A tangled record remains to indicate notes given by Barton, a $225 judgment secured by Wadhams and a complicated skein of legal maneuverings which may have led in part to Barton's downfall fourteen years later.

Other suits followed. The Vermonters knew almost nothing of Barton's brilliant war escapades and seemed to care less. He was soon in long and bitter litigation with Jonathan Allyn, Barton's first Town Representative, over land titles and damages.

While this case dragged on, more were entered against Barton by William Griswold and others, and small judgments awarded to them. Then at Irasburg, Allyn brought against Barton a suit for $3,000 and costs. Three referees appointed by the court to investigate were William Palmer of Danville, judge, Congressman and later Governor; Azarias Williams of Concord, substantial merchant, jurist and landowner; and James Whitelaw of Ryegate, Surveyor-General of Vermont.

This group recommended that Allyn should recover damages of $50.13 and costs of $51.10, and the court so ordered. But Barton, though probably well able to pay, refused to do so.

And so William Barton was remanded to jail. In a tort (or civil wrong), close jail execution was legal, then as now. But there was no jail in the vicinity, so Barton was taken in custody to Danville, where the log-built Caledonia County jail recently had been erected facing the green. It was 1811 and Barton was sixty-three years old. Here he remained confined to the "jail yard" until released through the generosity of the famed Frenchman, Lafayette, in 1825.

I was engaged in writing *Yankee Yarns* when I first heard of William Barton. He seemed such a likely and independent Yankee that I thought he would be good copy for a broadcast. To my surprise I found most librarians had never heard of him, and for records of his trails, tribulations and achievements there were almost none.

Barton was born in Warren, Rhode Island, in 1748 and after a grammar-school education was apprenticed by his father to a hat-maker. Bill Barton was a smart boy. He studied long and worked

hard, and by the time he was twenty-one and free to go about his own business he had a hat shop of his own, and had married Rhoda Carver of Middleboro, Massachusetts. They had two children and a good home.

Then one night as he was reading his copy of the *Providence Gazette* Barton saw a brief account of the battle on Bunker Hill. Feeling that the Yankees needed every fighting man they could get, he closed his shop, hurried to Boston and there was enlisted with General Artemus Ward's army in Cambridge. Soon he was defending the new fortifications at Dorchester Heights.

Barton proved to be an exceptionally daring soldier, led several successful raids into enemy lines, and kept morale high among the men. At Dorchester Heights he had his first glimpse of the great Washington, whom he idolized. When word was brought in December that his wife had given birth to a new baby son he named him George Washington Barton.

The British now were extending their activities to the shores of Rhode Island, and to forestall them the Americans built a small fort at Tiverton. The next problem was to find the right man to command it.

Israel Putnam suggested this native Rhode Islander, a man of spunk. So Barton was promoted and dispatched to Rhode Island. Sadness and shock came upon him when he saw what the British invaders had done to the lovely towns of Bristol, Portsmouth and Newport. When the redcoats had complained of the cold their commander at Newport, General Prescott, had pointed to the fine shade trees lining the streets. He sent his Hessians to rip up wooden sidewalks and grave markers for firewood.

All but two of Newport's fine churches were reduced to barracks or were used as stables. Prescott had his own headquarters in the John Bannister house, but suddenly decided to move into the country. He seized the fine farm of John Overing, a dignified Quaker who submitted in silence as Prescott moved into his home.

A few Britishers (who also had reason to hate Prescott) escaped from camp and were brought before Barton. He questioned them in detail about the Overing house and finally decided that, with luck, he could stage a raid and capture the General. Making no mention of his daring plan to other Yankee officers, he did speak quietly to his men. Every man in his command volunteered.

Choosing forty who were experienced with boats and could be trusted to keep mum, Barton made his plans. Five whaleboats were procured and provisioned. Eight men were assigned to each boat, Barton in the first one. On July 4, 1777, they shoved off in a raging gale that was whipping across Mount Hope Bay.

It was difficult rowing in the darkness and raging seas. They were drenched to the skin, weary and hungry, but after twenty-six hours on the storm-tossed waters the five boats made Hog Island, where the men rested. Ahead in the darkness they could see British campfires. Then Barton revealed to his men the full plan.

Landing a mile below the Overing house, which was guarded by only a few Britishers, Barton left part of his force to guard the boats and keep them in readiness for a quick departure. The others he led along a narrow path which stretched from the sea to the farmhouse on the hill. As expected, they were challenged by a sentry, but as the soldier lowered his musket he was caught in a cloak, gagged and bound. The house was surrounded, and Barton leaped up the front staircase. Bursting open a locked door, he found General Prescott sitting drunkenly on his bed, stark naked, vainly trying to pull on a pair of pants.

Dragged as he was down the stairs, he was rushed past a cut-over pasture, through underbrush to the waiting whaleboats. Quickly they shoved off, while bonfires were lighted on shore and alarm bells rang. A few bullets whizzed harmlessly over their heads.

Barton placed his distinguished prisoner in the bow of the whaleboat, where he could watch him. Finally he gave the shivering Prescott his own coat, and when they reached land, the General was rushed to the army barracks, was permitted a warm bath and a good breakfast. Later he was taken by carriage to Providence and on to Washington's headquarters in New York.

For this daring exploit, William Barton was promoted and given a vote of thanks by the Rhode Island Assembly. Congress gratefully awarded him a suitable inscribed, jeweled sword.

Shortly afterward, in May of 1779, when the British attacked

WM. BARTON

HATS

⌗An Account
of the
Daring Capture
of Gen. Prescott
by
Wm. BARTON
& his Troops
1777

BARTON
VERMONT

Your old friend
Lafayette

the village of Warren, Barton rode ahead of his troops to save the meetinghouse from being burned. But in the fighting he received a serious thigh wound and never fought in battle again.

Barton lay for weeks near death in his Warren home. Here he was recuperating when the French fleet under Count Rochambeau arrived. Barton was pleased to receive a visit from both the Admiral and the gallant Marquis de Lafayette, who became his lifelong friend.

Soon afterward Barton was elected to the Rhode Island legislature, was appointed a customs officer, made a colonel in the United States army and a general in the Rhode Island militia.

He settled down in Warren, but not for long. He knew many army men who had seen the beauties of unsettled Vermont and who talked endlessly of the timberlands and fertile fields. Along with Daniel Owen, Ira Allen and John Paul Jones, Barton soon appealed for a tract of Vermont's wild land, intending to call the new town "Providence."

William Barton's long years of confinement at Danville are passed off by some as a glorified vacation, an easy life, plenty of hunting and fishing, a comfortable room and visitors eager to hear the old man recount his wartime exploits.

A very different view of Barton's confinement emerges elsewhere, however. Although not locked inside the jail, he was confined to the "jail yard," which was marked by chains wrapped around trees one mile out of town on each of the five roads leading from Danville. Most of the prisoners, and perhaps Barton among them, worked out their keep or fines for neighborhood farmers, and reportedly the "pickings were exceedingly slim." Anyone furnishing liquor to prisoners was remanded to the jail yard himself.

Barton's various suits went on for some years even while he was a prisoner at Danville, and until 1814. The sums involved were small and Barton lost most though not all the cases. This same year, while jailed, Barton petitioned Congress, not for his release (though he said he was "confined within the liberties of the prison at Danville"), but for back pay and compensation for wounds received in the Revolution. The sum asked was £75/15/5. His petition concluded that age, infirmity, and his present situation

153

prevented his "defending his country against her ancient and inveterate enemy in the present contest" (the War of 1812). Repeatedly over the years he vainly petitioned the Vermont legislature for release.

Even the manner in which Barton accepted his final release is in doubt. During Lafayette's visit to Vermont in 1825 the Marquis is said to have asked in Montpelier about his old friend, William Barton. Told by General Isaac Fletcher of Lyndon of Barton's sad plight, Lafayette expressed sorrow and concern. Later, as his ship, *Brandywine*, left for France, he sent a personal draft to General Fletcher to defray Barton's debt.

Some reports said Barton bitterly contested this payment for his release — because he wanted vindication, not settlement. Others conjectured he was too pleased with his situation in Danville to want to leave. Still another version had it that Barton was wild with joy: "With what emotions of surprise and gratitude this intelligence was received . . . can be better imagined than described," wrote the Danville *North Star* some years after the memorable release. Other reports said that Barton rode the stage back to his family in Providence "tears in his eyes" and "singing Revolutionary songs all the way."

But to the historian, intrigued by the many hidden aspects of William Barton's strange tale, much still remains for conjecture. What lay behind this tragic and quixotic career? Remaining to be explained are these points:

1. Why did this famous hero desert his home and hearth for a howling wilderness, and there remain for thirty years separated from his apparently loving wife and children?

2. What manner of man was Barton to his Vermont neighbors that he neither wanted nor was granted offices or honors in the town he founded?

3. Why was this hero so little regarded by Vermonters and high-placed Americans generally that they permitted him to remain in jail for fourteen years?

4. Was it sloth or overweening pride which impelled Barton to default a paltry judgment in favor of jail?

Here is one construction which has been placed upon this amazing career:

When Barton departed from Rhode Island at forty-seven it was as a man not only bent on winning quick fortune but as one perhaps already seriously estranged from his family; already, perhaps, harboring the makings of megalomania.

In the rough frontier of northern Vermont perhaps his arrogant attitude and ruthless business methods led to loss of both friends and public respect. Jailed for refusing to pay a judgment, he had reached the limit of his horizon. Pride and stubbornness allowed neither retreat nor admission of wrong. Exoneration remained his only avenue of escape.

Those fourteen years in the Danville jail yard were not the easy retirement of an amiable, lazy old man who rather fancied being a character. It was a hard life. But harder for William Barton than the poverty and humiliation was the knowledge that there could be no deliverance except that of his dreams — the deliverance of public exoneration befitting a maligned national hero.

But did Lafayette sweep into Danville with gorgeous military retinue and bear Colonel Barton away in triumph? No, the Marquis

155

sent a check, discreetly and through channels to the proper authorities, to defray an ignominious debt. Bill Barton fought his release, this technical deliverance. But, an old man now, he knew there never would come the golden public acclaim which would free both him and his pride.

Quietly, defeated at last, he slipped back to his now alien home in Rhode Island, to his now-strange wife and family, to die there, decently. But in Vermont, in a sense, death had come to him, the rejected hero, twenty years before. And did not this long life really end at twenty-nine, that gloriously exciting night at Newport in 1777?

Soon after Barton's death, Catherine Williams's popular and adulatory *Biography of Revolutionary Heroes* was published in New York. Giving the full hero's treatment to William Barton's career, the author concludes in teary prose with her visit to the recently widowed Rhoda Barton in her quiet Providence home, of their gazing in hushed reverence together at the Colonel's portrait. Nowhere in her detailed biography, however, does Mrs. Williams even hint of William Barton's thirty-year Vermont interlude.

Rhoda Carver Barton was eighty when her husband died, and in the decade following, until her own demise in 1841, there is evidence that she, at least, enjoyed a modest pension, provided in its own good time by a grateful government.

Epilogue

THE STORY OF CLARENCE ADAMS, which led off this collection of strange goings-on, opens with the observation that "great mysteries seem to favor obscure beginnings, flourish in quiet settings." An outlander might glide casually over this remark, not realizing that for Vermonters it implies much more than it actually states. A denizen of the Green Mountains absorbs its connotation silently, perhaps lifting an eyebrow and maybe nodding his head almost imperceptibly, or even by slightly puckering his lips.

For we do live in quiet settings, and in them often watch events that evolve from beginnings as undefined as, near Labor Day, the fall of a leaf from the still-green branches of our favorite maple, or the look of the twigs as, in March, the sap invisibly rises within it. This same tranquillity, however, can often produce the unexpected. Therefore when even a native Vermonter claims he saw in the woods an animal that looked suspiciously like a panther, we do not remind him that the last panther killed in the state was shot in Barnard in 1881. Nor do we, when a sober and literate neighbor describes the shape and size of the Lake Champlain sea monster he saw from a cliff overlooking the Lake, discredit his testimony with disparaging arguments that impugn his veracity. (Although we may, if the story is especially rich, pursue the subject with a series of straightforward questions in a deadpan manner.)

Also, in out quiet settings, we realize that much is happening near by that does not necessarily meet the eye: On a cold Winter day, when snow is piled high and the visible universe seems still, we know that field mice very likely have dug a network of tunnels beneath the pathway we have shoveled to our door, and are scurrying through them only a few feet from where we stand. Thus it follows that Vermonters can live easily with mysteries; and it amuses us when, for example, we hear out-of-staters at Vermont's colleges complain of the oddities in their campus buildings. True, still to be explained are the antics in Northfield at the Norwich University library, where lights blink and doors slam at midnight, and books fall inexplicably from shelves with loud thuds. On the other hand, at Goddard College, in Plainfield, the ghost of a dead butler can be heard walking in an upstairs corridor of a girls' dormitory. (A faculty member, who said he did not believe in ghosts, reports that when he was in the building the name "Dawson" had constantly intruded upon his consciousness. Sure enough, a little research turned up the fact that years ago, when the dormitory was a private residence, there *had been* a butler and his name *was* Dawson and he *did* live in a room on that very corridor.) This type of information does not surprise us; we respond with the same solemn nod of understanding with which our money-digging forebears learned of the phantoms who guarded the treasure in Bristol.

Such unflappability is standard behavior, as witness the more extreme example offered by John P. Weeks of North Danville in 1838. He was twenty-six years old when, in the June of that year, he fell ill, claimed to have died and been taken to Paradise by two angels, given a horrifying glimpse of Hell, and finally returned to his deathbed, thereupon to be brought back to life again. John wrote an account of his journey, somehow making it seem less incredible by pausing to give a Vermont hill-farmer's view of sheer heaven:

> The climate in Paradise is delightful and healthy. No clouds, winds, or unpleasant storms appear. The air is always alike, neither hot nor cold. A gentle breeze blows from the northwest, sweeter than honey. The land is perfectly level, the grass perhaps half an inch high, with neither trees, stumps nor stones to mar the pleasantness.

Fifteen of Weeks's friends and neighbors at his bedside, among them doctors and clergy, witnessed his apparent death and recovery. They signed a statement recounting what they had seen, including testimony of observable physical actions by Weeks during the crisis. They also recorded their belief in his experience by declaring him to be "a man of sound mind and good understanding, a man of truth and veracity, Christian character, industrious farmer, and faithful citizen, esteemed by all who know him."

Skeptics who doubt this statement should remember that Vermonters do not glibly dismiss the testimony of their neighbors about what they have seen or done. And some Vermonters have done some amazing things: It was a young man from Sharon, in the east-central part of the state, who in 1823 was told in a vision of the golden plates on which was inscribed the Book of Mormon. (He was Joseph Smith, and his greatest convert was Brigham Young, from Whitingham down in the southeast corner, who led the Mormons on to Utah.)

The native bent for accepting the mysterious and the unexpected has not lost its vitality in recent years. In the northern Vermont town of Greensboro I own a few acres of land that look across a narrow valley toward the town cemetery. About six miles farther north lies Craftsbury, where Alfred Hitchcock made *The Trouble with Harry*, one of his chilling suspense movies, in the early 1950's. Harry's trouble was that he was dead, and a few leading citizens in that bucolic setting were having great difficulty in safely getting rid of Harry's body. But that is not my tale in this instance. My tale concerns the body of a man buried in the Greensboro town cemetery in the 1880's. One night in 1968 somebody opened his grave and dug down to his coffin, carefully removing all the dirt to a tarpaulin spread near by. The village was mystified when the deed was discovered in the clear light of morning. Who opened the grave? Nobody knows. Why dig it up so carefully? Nobody knows. The man had no descendants living in Greensboro; only a few old-timers could vaguely recall the family. Had a gold name-plate bearing the dead man's name been fastened onto the coffin, and was the digger trying to find it? Or more — had the digger found an old letter or diary that told of a bag of money secretly lowered into the grave at the time of the burial? No one knows to this day.

Vermonters are familiar with the unfamiliar, at ease with the unforeseen, unmoved by a fuss that would upset our city cousins.

If you have responded like a native to the tales in this book — and enjoyed them perhaps both eyebrows lifted and lips pursed a bit — you have as my parting gift the Greensboro mystery and the poltergeist in Northfield as starters for your own collection.

Mischief in these mountains is occurring all the time. It sometimes escapes our attention because it is done so slyly. This is no laughing matter.

Montpelier   Charles T. Morrissey, *Director*
January 1970   *Vermont Historical Society*

Mischief in the Mountains

$\mathcal{T}$he $\mathcal{W}$riters

RICHARD SANDERS ALLEN, who lives with his wife at Ballston Lake, N.Y., is considered the national authority on covered bridges. He has written many magazine articles and several books on the subject, and in 1963–1964 did Guggenheim Fellowship work in the field. He is intimately familiar with Vermont history, and has particular interest in postal and railroad lore, as well as such mysteries as the Boorn case.

The late ALTON HALL BLACKINGTON, a native of Rockland, Maine was best known as the author of the *Yankee Yarns* books and for the Boston newspaper column by the same name which he wrote for many years at his home in Beverly Farms, Mass. He was an accomplished photographer and lectured widely on New England folklore.

LAWRENCE G. BLOCHMAN, who terms himself a reformed newspaperman, worked in California, Japan, Malaysia, Indonesia, India, France and Guatemala before turning to "fiction without headlines" in 1929. Except for a year in Hollywood and five with the Office of War Information, he has been a freelance writer ever since. He boasts the publication of forty-odd books, many of them mysteries, some 200 short stories and articles, and six movies. He often summers in Vermont, where six of his books were written, and lives in New York with his Parisian-born wife. Best known, perhaps, are his books on Dr. Daniel Webster Coffee, the pathologist-detective.

JANE CLARK BROWN, who lives in South Burlington with her husband and three sons, is a native of Burlington and a graduate of Syracuse University's School of Art. Her weekly political cartoons appearing in the Essex Junction *Suburban List* have won special commendation by the New England Press Association.

GEORGE G. CONNELLY, lawyer, college teacher (at Annapolis, Maryland) and columnist, is a Cornell graduate who has practiced law in Rochester and New York City, later teaching at the University of Georgia and Williams College. His column, "Professor-at-Large," has appeared for more than a decade in the Pittsfield, Mass. *Berkshire Eagle*.

JANET C. GREENE, a graduate of Stanford University, a reporter and feature writer for metropolitan papers on the West Coast, she later did Foreign Broadcast Intelligence work. In 1944 she was married to Stephen Greene.

She is a contributing editor to *Vermont Life* Magazine, is vice-president of Greenemont Books and senior editor for The Stephen Greene Press, and the author of two books of epitaphs.

STEPHEN GREENE is a Boston native and Harvard graduate who worked as newspaper correspondent in Tokyo and Paris, and during the War for the Broadcast Intelligence Service. He moved with his family to Vermont in 1945, where he has been a bookseller, publisher, state legislator, town official and *Vermont Life* Magazine senior editor. His special interests include conservation education, forestry and agriculture.

WESLEY S. GRISWOLD, a resident of Los Angeles, has an extensive background in newspaper and magazine feature writing, including staff work with *Popular Science* and *The New Yorker*. His writing, strong in railroad lore, includes the book, *Train Wreck*, published in 1969. He is an accomplished pianist, collects old ship prints and Chinese porcelain.

WALTER R. HARD, JR., who collaborated with Stephen Greene in the tale of Chester's Gentleman Burglar, is a Vermont native who grew up in Manchester, graduated from Dartmouth College, has been editor of *Vermont Life* Magazine since 1950, and now lives in Burlington with his wife and two sons. He served with the Mountain Infantry during World War II and thereafter worked as a reporter in Vermont. His interests include Vermont historical happenings of the more bizarre type.

RALPH NADING HILL, a Burlington native and a graduate of Dartmouth College, is an authority on Lake Champlain and steamboat history. His published books include the history of his college, *Sidewheeler Saga, Contrary Country, Window on the Sea, The Mad Doctor's Drive* and *Yankee Kingdom*. His detailed knowledge of Vermont extends from its earliest history, here evidenced in the John Graye story, to present-day work in the field of educational television. He is a senior editor of *Vermont Life* Magazine and a trustee of the Shelburne Museum.

MURRAY HOYT as a boy spent his summers away from his native Worcester, Mass. on the shores of Lake Champlain. Later he graduated from Middlebury College, taught and coached sports in New York state, until beginning in 1930 a long career as freelance magazine writer. He and his family built and operated for twenty-five years the Lake Champlain resort of Owl's Head Harbor, which is still in the family. He is the author of many articles and books in the fields of sports, nature and humor, is a senior editor of *Vermont Life* Magazine. His home is in Middlebury.

LOUIS A. LAMOUREUX graduated from Yale University, where he majored in Government, and years later reclaimed his Vermont heritage, for a time with the Northeastern Vermont Development Association. He now is deep in Peacham town affairs, serving as town clerk and treasurer, treasurer of the school district, as trustee of Peacham Academy, president of the Peacham Historical Society, treasurer of Peacham Cemetery (and its countless trust funds), chairman of the town planning commission, fund-raiser for the Peacham Library and publicist for most local activities. Between times he is a real estate broker and collects Vermont historical anecdotes which find their way into freelance writing, such as the Dale Curse story.

LESLIE C. MOORE's teaching duties (English) at St. Johnsbury Academy and summer attendance at the Bread Loaf School of English in Ripton have left little time for further study of Vermont eccentricity. He graduated from Harvard in 1964 and traveled in Europe and the Middle East before returning to his native St. Johnsbury, where he and his wife now live.

CHARLES T. MORRISSEY, director of the Vermont Historical Society and professor of history at the University of Vermont, has been associated with the Oral History projects related to the administrations of Presidents Truman, Kennedy and Johnson. He edits the Vermont Historical Society's quarterly magazine and its regular newsletter, is a member of the Vermont Board of Historic Sites and is a *Vermont Life* Magazine columnist.

ROCKWELL STEPHENS, a skiing visitor to Vermont since 1930, moved with his wife to South Woodstock in 1953. He has been a newspaper sports and feature writer, ski equipment manufacturer, teacher and writer of two books on skiing. He now does freelance writing, assists in a bookshop operation and cultivates his hundred-acre woodlot.

NOEL C. STEVENSON was born in Sacramento and returned to California from a boyhood in Utah to attend Pacific Coast College and for admission to the California bar in 1944. Except for the period 1951 to 1954 when he served as district attorney of Sutter County, he has practiced private law. His interests mainly are California, Vermont (where he has a part-time home), historical and genealogical research, beachcombing, writing and the law. He is the author of a number of books on legal subjects and on genealogical research methods. His home is in Santa Rosa.

SYLVESTER L. VIGILANTE, after many years as head of the New York Public Library's American History Room, retired in 1953, and until 1958 was bibliographer for the New York Historical Society. He is an outstanding authority on the bad men and peace officers of the West. He first was lured to Vermont by the Long Trail, bought a summer place here in 1930 and spends much of the year there with his wife. His home is just outside New York City.

Further Notes

The Man Who Wouldn't Be Bored: Rumors, fanned in large part by the Hearst press, that Clarence Adams had indeed feigned death and escaped, persisted in Vermont for many years and, indeed, still are believed by some. But so great was the public speculation, that open (and some secret) hearings were held during 1905 and 1906 by special legislative committee meetings in Bellows Falls, Windsor, and other towns. In part, the hearings examined possible laxity in the management of Windsor State Prison, where, besides the possibility of Adams's connived escape, there was the rumor of state-purchased coal disappearing in large lots, and the scandalous freedoms said to have been accorded the husband-murderer, Mary Rogers, before her demise. She was the last woman to be executed in Vermont.

At a hearing on November 1st, 1905, Dr. J. D. Brewster testified that he had personally certified to Adams's death and that he believed there was "no foundation to the story" of Adams still being alive. Undertaker Lyman F. Cabot also swore he had injected the body with "two quarts or more" of embalming fluid, whereas a gill would kill a man. He further testified "yes" to the question, whether he understood the body was that of Adams and stated that "he had a sore on his limb that might be from a shot." Oddly enough, the shoe salesman, John Greenwood, who was widely quoted as having seen Adams in Montreal, apparently was never called upon to testify on this point.

In 1960 the late Fred V. Perkins, who had operated the Cavendish General Store for many years, wrote that he had been present when Adams was buried, after removal from the crypt where the body had been held until spring. Sexton Sanders had said, Perkins reported, that Adams's relatives had asked him to open the casket and identify the corpse, since he had known Adams. "That's Adams, all right," Sanders said, according to Perkins's letter.

Did the Sailor Die? There have been no new developments nor has fresh evidence been disclosed in the mystery of John Graye since the publication of this account in 1966. General opinion in Vermont tends to support the position that the lead tube and its enigmatic contents were among the many historical hoaxes so popular in the 19th Century; and probably were fabricated by a practical joker friend of the Dr. Baxter, the antiquarian enthusiast who purchased the tube and parchment from the men who dug it up.

Although Mr. Hill's examination of the whole body of evidence appears to result in a negative conclusion, the story, like that of Human Hibernation, contains enough elements of plausibility so that many still believe it may be true. In a similar vein, there are Vermonters who refuse to disbelieve the human footprints found many years ago and still evident on the side of a rock ledge at the foot of Cranberry Meadow Pond in the town of Calais.

Fall of the House of Hayden: Offering further proof of the virulence of Mercie Dale's curse, is the following data which came to light following publication of the Hayden story in 1963:

The elegant furnishings of the Hayden Mansion actually were sold with the house in 1922 to Canadian purchasers. But bad luck followed even the Hayden chattels. The Canadians crated up the mansion's remaining furniture, including a rosewood piano, and sent it back by rail to Canada. On the way, however, the train was derailed and one of the freight cars rolled down an embankment, completely destroying its contents. This, of course, was the carload of furniture from Vermont.

The Deep Frozen Folks of Farmer Morse: The staying power of Farmer Morse's inspired story can be shown in many ways, including the inquiries about human hibernation practices in Vermont repeatedly received from medical research centers in various parts of the world.

The tale is found in unexpected media also. During the autumn of 1964, devotees of the newspaper comic strip *Dick Tracy* were gripped by a fresh episode concerning the aviatrix, Lita Flite, who, missing since 1937, had been found frozen into a chunk of Arctic ice. Confronting the mad scientist, Dr. Ludwick Frost, Dick Tracy barked: "Are you implying that after all these years this individual can be restored to life?"

"There is no technical problem," the bearded doctor affirmed. But the outcome of his resuscitation efforts was lost to view in subsequent strips in a confusion of Red spies, gangsters and two-way wrist televisions. At the time, *Vermont Life* expressed confidence, however, that the Doctor would bring it off.

"Dunk her gently in a wooden trough of warm water," the Magazine counseled. "That's the way they did it in Vermont."

Folklore investigator Rowland Wells Robbins, the Lincoln, Massachusetts resident who tracked the Human Hibernation tale to its originator, is also an archeologist whose important projects have included the uncovering and restoration of America's first iron works in Saugus, Mass., restoration of the early powder mills in Delaware, excavations at Crown Point and restorations at Sleepy Hollow. He also has done extensive research into the enigma of the many underground beehive structures which are prevalent in parts of New England, including Vermont, and which some believe were built by pre-Columbian Celtic monks.

The Sad Fate of John O'Neil: True yet improbable happenings, such as the tribulations of Whitehall, N.Y. liquor dealer, John O'Neil, often are completely lost to public knowledge in the span of just a few years. Frequently they are uncovered accidentally, as was Professor Connolley's tale. During some otherwise conventional legal research Noel C. Stevenson, Esq., happened upon the "Strange Wedding of the Widow Ward," (see below), in similar fashion.

Subsequent to the 1968 publication of John O'Neil's sad story, it came to light that for many years he had operated in Whitehall an emporium named the Temple of Economy. He was described locally as "one of Whitehall's most public-spirited citizens," yet he was known as something of an eccentric. One of his quirks was the insistence that a brass bed always be kept set up in the parlor of his home, in order to embarrass and discourage his daughter from entertaining suitors.

At this writing it has not yet been determined what part of his heavy sentence John O'Neil actually served.

The Vampire's Heart: Although apparently entirely fictitious, the original recounting of the Woodstock vampire illustrates considerable narrative skill in that its tracing is purposely obscured by framing it as a story within a story, by the credibility lent to it in staging the action at a true and familiar setting (Woodstock's boat-shaped Green), and the interjection of the names of attesting witnesses who were prominent citizens (but at the time safely long-deceased). The tale, together with the Human Hibernation yarn, further supports the author's note that Vermonters of the era were particularly partial to stories of the macabre, not to say the ghoulish, and that credibility often was enhanced with paramedical knowledge of the day, mixed with ancestral superstitions.

Wildly at variance with the scene conjured up by this tale is the look of the Green today, where a massive hostelry, the new Woodstock Inn, has been erected by the international Rockresorts, a Rockefeller consortium.

Money, Injustice and Bristol Bill: The impact of counterfeit money upon American life a century and more ago, now is largely forgotten. At first it was largely coins, because paper money was too difficult to validate and did not carry inherent value anyway. "Death to Counterfeiters" commonly appeared on bank notes at a later date, attesting to the seriousness of the problem, which was compounded by the probability that issuing banks often had little metal to stand behind their notes.

Counterfeiting as a career (not always a happy one) is noted also in the extension of Stephen Boorn's biography, as the data below show. It enters also into the story of Reuben Harmon's mint (not in this volume), which was located in Rupert, Vermont, and where copper pennies were minted by Vermont authority during the Republic's 14-year existence. Harmon's little mint on Hagar's Brook, mainly using machinery secured in Connecticut, put out a variety of Vermont pennies from 1785 to 1788. Later, in 1800, some of this gear, the roller to form the copper planchets and the screwpowered stamping die press, was found on the slopes of Mt. Anthony in Rupert, presumably abandoned and destroyed by counterfeiters, who, like latter-day moonshiners (not in Vermont, of course) were harassed constantly by the law, which was kept vigilant because of unaccustomed public support.

There has been conjecture as to what base metals could have been used in 1800 to produce false pennies at a profit, although by 1793 Vermont copper was being mined and smelted in quantity across the state in Strafford.

Bristol Bill was long a favorite of the *National Police Gazette*, the nation's rowdiest and most popular scandal sheet. More useful, if less entertaining sources for this study are the contemporary issues of the St. Johnsbury *Caledonian* and the Danville *North Star.* However, press coverage of the Groton Bank naturally suffered from the competition of the simultaneous trial, one of the juiciest of the century, of Harvard's Professor Webster for the murder of his colleague, Dr. Parkman. Later in the decade Warburton was the subject of a pamphlet biography (which changed its title with each edition) by a Boston reporter named George Thompson, who wrote under the pen-name of "Greenhorn." More recently the late Herbert Asbury, in *All Around the Town*, and Jack Dunne, in a factual article in the St. Johnsbury *Caledonian-Record*, have given Bill some richly deserved attention. s.g.

Eighteen-Hundred-and-Froze-to-Death: The year 1816 was not the only freezing time in Vermont (and much of the north country), of course. There was a succession of alarmingly cold years, extending into the 1830's, which probably were caused, it is conjectured now, by the presence in the upper atmosphere of heavy dust clouds produced by gigantic volcanic explosions elsewhere in the world. The bad luck and famine these years produced in what the new Vermonters had thought was a promised land, triggered heavy waves of migration from Vermont to the opening lands in the West.

An examination of the *Vermont Almanac* for 1816 shows these questionable forecasts: for June; "Fine growing weather." for

171

July; "Good weather for farmers," and for August; "Pleasant weather for some time." With no apology at all, the *Almanac* was back in 1817 with similar optimistic proposals.

The Boorn Mystery: The legal aspects of this true story have had more profound effects nationally than any other criminal matter brought to justice in Vermont. Many states, including Vermont, as a result changed their laws to avoid such a near-tragedy as threatened Stephen Boorn. Some states now refuse to accept pleas of guilty in first-degree murder cases.

Much has been written about the Boorn case over the years including *The Trial and Confession of Jesse and Stephen Boorn for the Murder of Russell Colvin,* by the Hon. Leonard Sargent, Manchester, 1873; *The Boorn Mystery, An Episode from the Judicial Annals of Vermont,* by the Hon. Sherman R. Moulton, Montpelier, 1937; and *The Return of Russell Colvin,* by John Spargo, Bennington, 1945. The story has been told nationally, also, in Edmund Lester Pearson's classic *Studies in Murder.* By some accounts Stephen Boorn's quixotic confession is evidence the third-degree was imposed. Better study appears to prove there was no physical coercion, although psychological pressures probably were strong.

Following the publication of Mr. Allen's account of the Boorn Mystery in 1959, this interesting data came to light:

On August 6, 1860 Convict #4913 was confined at the Ohio Penitentiary in Columbus for "making and passing counterfeit coins." He served to the end of his sentence, November 23, 1864. He was listed as a Vermont native; he could neither read nor write; he was 75 years old, and his name was Jesse M. Boorn, (alias Bowen).

Here is more on Jesse's last years: The 1866 volume, *Narrative of Spies, Scouts and Detectives,* contains a report by U. S. Marshall Harry Newcomer that, on suspicion being presented, he made the acquaintance of an old blacksmith living on a small farm near Burton Square. He introduced himself as a manufacturer of and dealer in counterfeit money, and gained his confidence (and later conviction). The point of interest here, however, is Newcomer's further quoting of Boorn:

"Early in life he and his brother had murdered their brother-in-law in Vermont, but, he said, he had been saved from the gallows by a man being found who bore a strong resemblance to the murdered man and who was induced to swear that he was the man supposed to be killed."

The Strange Wedding of the Widow Ward: Descendents of William Ward, following the 1962 publication of this story, evidenced the sentiment that their ancestor had been maligned, to a degree, for having left his comely widow in such exposed circumstances. Mr. Ward, they reported, was an early settler of Newfane and that town's 1780 representative to the Vermont Assembly. The adjoining town of Wardsboro was named in his honor. Mr. Ward's unexpected death while on a fur-trading trip to Canada was the reason his estate and his widow were left in jeopardy.

The solution to this Vermont legalistic tangle found by Moses Joy and his bride was tested at least one other time. Another widow was married naked in Westminster about the same period. According to reports, this ceremony took place on the roof of a house, the bride stationed beside a dormer window, her natural state concealed by a curtain pulled out from the window.

Further research into the Ward case by co-author Stevenson in Joy and Ward family genealogies confirmed the facts given in this story, as did U. S. Census records and those of Moses Joy's estate probation. The latter shows that Hannah, widowed a second time, spent the sum of $12 for a funeral dress.

The Money Diggers: Probably there will never be an ending to Vermonters' interest in buried treasure. Among the state's long-standing legends is that a Captain Stephen Mallett in the late 1700's settled on the bay near Burlington which now bears his name, that he was a retired pirate, ran a rough tavern, and, before his death, buried great treasures on Coates Island. Marker trees which pointed to the trove were learned of many years later — and only after they had been destroyed in a storm. That nobody really forgets buried treasure was demonstrated in 1965 when in France, the descendants of Jean-Pierre Mallett, who died in 1818 in nearby Winooski (by their statement), laid claim against the U. S. Treasury for the sum of $512 million, which presumably is the value of Stephen Mallett's as yet undiscovered hoard.

173

Odd Men Out: There are few tangible evidences today of the Vermont eccentrics here delineated by Mr. Moore, except for Joseph Battell's Bread Loaf Inn, which now houses the Middlebury College Summer School of English and Writers' Conference. Columbus Smith's ornate, Italianate pile still stands in the remote reaches of Salisbury. However, the resident beneficiaries of Mr. Smith's restrictive bequest are living in a large wooden ell built onto the stone mansion.

The Case of the Rejected Hero: The laws that allowed the jailing of Col. William Barton for fourteen years because of a debt, substantially are in force in Vermont today, albeit a man cannot be jailed for *simple* debt. It must be a tort or "wrong," and today it is very seldom invoked. If such a close jail execution now is rendered, the prisoner does not have the one-mile radius jail-yard freedom accorded to Col. Barton. In 90 days, however, he may take the poor debtor's oath and be freed. But in that case his assets, if any, will be seized to satisfy the judgment.

Research data concerning Colonel Barton's career in Vermont were contributed to Mr. Blackington's story by Tennie Gaskill Toussaint of Danville and Noel C. Stevenson, Esq. now of Santa Rosa, California.